1 YEAR IN THE GREAT COMMANDMENT

THE LOVE JOURNAL

52 Weeks To Cultivate A Heart For God & Reflect His Love To Others

SCOTT ANDREW WILLIAMS

Kingdom Hope Ink
P.O. Box 2907
Costa Mesa, CA 92628
KingdomHope.Ink

ISBN 978-1-7365425-0-7 (paperback)
ISBN 978-1-7365425-1-4 (hardcover)
ISBN 978-1-7365425-2-1 (digital)

First Edition: January 2021

CONTENTS

INTRODUCTION

We tend to make matters of faith extremely complicated. There are the theologies of this and that, the dos and don'ts, the *begats* and the *shalts*. It can feel like there are too many things to remember, too many to heed, too many to wrap our heads around. These can result in a sense of confusion, overwhelm, and paralysis.

There are tons of libraries of books filled with guidance and theologies. Don't get me wrong. These authors and theologians have provided us with incredible value. The net effect for many however can be that faith can be too complicated to follow. In the face of so many things to do and learn, we can become apathetic.

Things were actually quite similar in the days of Jesus. A number of human traditions had been built up around the Word of God. There were traditions and commentaries that constructed a "*fence*" around the laws of God. Consequently, there was a whole layer beyond what God was asking of them so that they might not even come close to committing an infraction against God.

While the intent may have been good, these were not actually from God. The complexity of it all meant that the heart of God's desire for the people was lost at times. Instead of eagerly striving to be the people God was calling them to be, the focus was on avoidance of wrongdoing.

One day a man approached Jesus in a bid to entrap him. He asked Jesus which was the greatest of all the commandments. Given the complexity of their faith, laws, and traditions they were sure to catch him in His response. Many would have been snared by this ploy. Others might have contrived some very complex discourse to hedge their bets. Yet others might have avoided the line of questioning entirely.

As is often the case, Jesus charted his own course. He offers simple yet profound wisdom.

> "'*Love the Lord your God with all your heart and with all your soul and with all your mind.' This is the first and greatest commandment. And the second is like it: 'Love your neighbor as yourself.' All the Law and the Prophets hang on these two commandments.*" Matthew 22:37-40

Jesus responds with not one, but two commandments that are inextricably connected. First, love God with everything that you have. Second, love others. There is no command in scripture that is unbound from these.

We are to respond to the Creator, Sustainer, and Redeemer with wholehearted love. This God loves all humanity. He loves those we know and those we do not. He loves those we like and those we do not. If we love Him then we will love the things that He loves.

At its core, this is the response of faith. It is **very** simple. Love God. Love Others.

This does not negate the depth or mystery of the faith. Nevertheless, it brings us back to the essence of what God looks for from humans that decide to follow Him. While there is still more to discover and explore, the heart of what God calls humans to is contained in this "great commandment."

Neither does this simplicity make things easy. Any self-aware person realizes that they have a tendency to prioritize self over God. Any person that lives in community knows the challenge of interacting with, let alone caring for, other people. The great commandment is simple yet quite challenging. In fact, some of us may be ready to give up on God or people.

Don't give up though. Yes, this can be difficult. Yes, it is easier said than done. Yes, there is a part of you that draws you away from this way of living.

I have a secret to share with you. These are not actually inconsistent with who you are. **You were actually created to walk in these ways.** You have the image of God inside of you. You were crafted to love and glorify the Lord. You were designed to reflect His love to the world. You were blessed so that you might be a blessing to the world. You were created with a purpose that is built on these principles.

So, yes, faith can be really complicated. But at the end of the day, the heart of it comes down to merely two things - two very simple things. Love God and love others.

This journal is meant to take you on a journey to explore these basic yet profound ideas. The goal is to progressively deepen your love for the Almighty God and the neighbors that you find yourself surrounded with.

Each week has been designed to exercise and strengthen your love muscles. Like any workout, if you just engage here and there the impact will be diminished. If you commit to authentically and routinely engaging, however, I believe you will see your heart open up and transformed further.

Would you be willing to commit the next 52 weeks to chase after a more profound love for God and neighbor? Would you be willing to risk and see what happens when you do? Would you be willing to more intentionally pursue what Jesus deems the greatest commandment? God has called. I hope you will answer.

May the Lord bless your pursuit and work in, through, and around you on this journey.

HOW TO USE
THIS JOURNAL

This journal is meant to take you through 52 weeks of devotions. It alternates the emphasis between loving God and loving others. Each week has a particular focus meant to challenge you and help you grow. It includes a verse of the week, a devotion, scripture readings, and reflection questions. There is also space for setting goals, prayer requests, and journaling.

Each week you will spend time working through the week's devotion. Starting with week one, you can embark on a journey to more deeply love God and neighbors.

I recommend that you start the devotion at the beginning of the week, each week to build a good rhythm. Ideally, you spend time in it throughout the week in order to truly concentrate on and ponder the scriptures and focus of the week. This is more likely to produce the desired results than merely binging the week's content in a single sitting.

Write the dates for the week so you can track progress. If you somehow get thrown off and miss a week, don't give up. Just pick up where you left off and continue pursuing this worthy goal of responding to the greatest commandment.

VERSE OF THE WEEK

I recommend that you read the verse of the week daily. Consider writing it down in a place you spend a significant amount of time. You could also try to memorize the passage each week. No matter your approach, allow God's word to speak to you and work on your heart throughout the week.

DEVOTIONAL THOUGHT

Read the devotional thought for the week. While it will not take but a few minutes to read, find a time where you can have the space to ponder or meditate on the ideas. Write down in the journal any ideas that stick out to you together with any things that God is speaking to you.

READING PLAN

The Love Journal will take you through the entire New Testament and the Psalms. This will take an average of five minutes per day if you space them out through the week. Do not merely read the words on the page or screen. Watch for what is happening. Listen to what God is speaking to you. Reflect on what this means for your life and faith.

REFLECT

Each week includes several reflection questions to help you process the theme for the week. Take the time to contemplate the questions and write out responses. If you need more space, you can use the journaling section for additional space.

MY WEEKLY GOALS

After reading the devotional thought at the beginning of the week, set some goals and activities for yourself for the week. These will be broken out into our two focal points: Love God and Love Neighbor.

Goal: what outcome or result would you like to see?
This might look like a goal along the lines of "I want to be more passionate for God" or "I want to be more tender with my spouse." Set goals for the week. Check in during the course of the week. Be sure to revisit at the end to see where you made progress.

Activity: what action will you undertake to move you closer to your goals?
This might look like an action such as "Listen to worship music for 30 minutes a day" or "Buy a meal for a person in need." Don't just write them down. Make time to follow through and do these activities.

PRAYERS

This journal can help guide your prayers as well. There are a few ways that you can engage in this.

Daily Prayers

Each day, you can pray the morning and evening prayers. These are intended to frame the start and end of your day. They only take a few minutes but can make a significant difference in your intention and awareness each day. See the specific details in the Daily Prayers section below.

Weekly Prayers

Praise

As Jesus begins His famous Disciple's Prayer (or The Lord's Prayer) with "Hallowed be your name", so we want to commence with adoration for the Almighty Lord. Make a list of things that you would like to praise Him for. You can include recognition of God's greatness as well as blessings that you are grateful for.

Personal Prayers

Write down some prayers for ways that you want to see God move in your own life. While you may ask God for your necessities, pray also that He shows up in your life and move in transformative ways.

Prayers for Others

As prayers are not simply a personal wish list, invite Jesus to move in the lives of your neighbors as well. Pray that His Kingdom comes and His will be done in their lives. Pray for their needs. Perhaps ask Him how He might be calling you to collaborate with Him as He answers those prayers for others.

JOURNAL

The book provides space for you to write notes and journal your thoughts as well. You might include raw thoughts as you process the focus for the week, scriptures that stand out to you, or the words that God speaks to you. You can also use it to ponder what is happening in your life and to petition Jesus to move in very specific ways. You could, of course, use it for sermon notes as well. This space is yours to reflect upon and record how you can better love God and love others.

HOW TO USE IN SMALL GROUPS

This journal is primarily aimed at individual use. However, you might consider meeting with a friend or small group to converse and reflect together. You could discuss the reflection questions, scripture readings, or what God is speaking to and working in you.

A meeting might look like this:

1. Pray to invite God's presence into your gathering. Ask Him to open up your hearts and minds to the ways that He would want to transform you.

2. Read the devotional thought together. Start with the passage from Scripture and then read the devotional thought.

3. Dialogue through the discussion questions. While you might keep certain details private, especially when it comes to struggles with others, you can talk through the sentiment, nonetheless. Beyond the questions, consider any resistance you might be feeling, what the root of that is, what God would call you to, and how this practically applies to your life.

4. Share about your weekly goals and the ways that you see God moving.

5. Share your praises, personal prayer requests, and prayers for others. Then, spend some time in prayer together.

OTHER NOTES

Take note that there are additional sections at the end as well. These offer ideas for loving your neighbor, a place to list the people you are praying for this year, blessings you celebrate God for, and next steps.

May the Lord use this journal to mold you further into His image. May you open up your heart to allow Him to work in and through you.

DAILY
PRAYERS

Pray these prayer daily.

Start your day with the Morning Prayer, asking God to move and to give you the courage to step out in faith.

End your day with the Evening Prayer, reflecting on and praising God for how he showed up. We encourage you to record or jornal each day the various ways that you see God move in order to celebrate now and in the future.

PRAY WHEN YOU RISE
MORNING PRAYER

Our Father, I pause to praise your name. You are the One, True God. I am amazed that you - the Creator of the Universe - would look upon me. Your might far surpasses all others. Your goodness is more than I can comprehend. I declare that you are the Lord of Heaven and Earth. I proclaim the beautiful name of Jesus Christ.

I recall the countless ways you have moved in the past. You are so so good! Your grace is astounding. Your mighty works are awe inspiring. Your peace is comforting even in the darkest times. Your light brings joy that transcends circumstances.

Lord, I ask you to help me today. I call upon you to provide for my needs. As you have assisted your people throughout the centuries, I ask that you would care for me today.

As I look to the day ahead, I ask that you would be working in the following areas of my life. **[Pray for some specific areas in your life for today]**

Where I am weak, be strong.
Where I am weary, revive me.
Where I am sick, heal me.
Where I am fearful, encourage me.

Beyond my own needs, I ask that you be moving here on Earth. I want to see your Kingdom come. May you be working in the lives of those around me.
[Pray for those you will encounter today & others that God puts on your heart]

May you, the Author of Salvation, collaborate with me to write my story.
 I invite you to move in my life today.
Help me to step out in faith.
 I invite you to move in my life today.
Give me the discernment to identify opportunities to shine your light to the world.
 I invite you to move in my life today.
Mold my heart that I might love all those I encounter as you do.
 I invite you to move in my life today.
May I be interruptible by your Kingdom's work.
 I invite you to move in my life today.
Grant me the courage to boldly leap even when fearful.
 I invite you to move in my life today.
Let your power - the same power that created the universe and raised Jesus from the grave -
be at work within me to accomplish mighty acts in your name.
 I invite you to move in my life today.
May my thoughts and actions glorify you.
 I invite you to move in my life today.
May your will be done in my life and in this world.
 I invite you to move in my life today.

As you move today, open my eyes to see you. May I see your beauty, know your grandeur, and
feel your presence.
May I experience the things of your Kingdom and recognize your hand in them.

Spirit go before me.
Emmanuel walk beside me.
Father God stand behind me.
Surround me with Your presence, oh Lord.
Move in me, through me, and around me this day.

+ *In the name of the Father, and the Son, and the Holy Spirit. Amen.*

EVENING PRAYER

Lord Jesus,

As I reflect on the day, I am grateful for the opportunity to live in your creation. You are majestic and I'm honored to have a relationship with you.

Please forgive me for any ways I fell short of living in your image today. Thank you for your mercy and your love that persists even when I make mistakes.
Cultivate in me a kind and compassionate heart that desires to extend the same forgiveness to those that have wronged me.

Help me to recognize the ways in which you revealed yourself this day.
[Reflect on how God moved today]

I celebrate how you acted today. Help me to trust that you are working even when I cannot see it. Continue to reveal your goodness to me.

Even in the midst of the challenges I face today, I will trust in you. Help me when my faith wavers.

I praise you God for your many blessings.
    Lord Jesus Christ be glorified.
I praise you God for your patience with me.
    Lord Jesus Christ be glorified.
I praise you God for the ways you moved today, for those I have seen and those not yet visible to me.
    Lord Jesus Christ be glorified.

I praise you God for the future hope of a restored world which was accomplished on the cross.

      Lord Jesus Christ be glorified.

I praise you God because of your goodness, your grace, and your love.

      Lord Jesus Christ be glorified.

This night may you prepare me for the journey ahead tomorrow. Transform me further into a true human being created in your image, reflecting your glory to the world. May I be courageous enough to trust you in the valleys and humble enough to praise you on the mountain tops.

As I lie down tonight, may I find comfort in your hope and rest in your peace.

+ *In the name of the Father, and the Son, and the Holy Spirit. Amen.*

WEEKLY
DEVOTIONS

ALL IN

Date: _____

VERSE OF THE WEEK

Y ou shall love the Lord your God with all your heart, and with all your soul, and with all your might.

DEUTERONOMY 6:5

READING PLAN

- ☐ Luke 1:1-25
- ☐ Luke 1:26-56
- ☐ Luke 1:57-80
- ☐ Luke 2:1-21
- ☐ Luke 2:22-52
- ☐ Luke 3:1-22
- ☐ Psalm 1
- ☐ Psalm 2

DEVOTIONAL THOUGHT

Read Deuteronomy 6:1-9

Whether a new hobby, a house project, or making a promise, I like to tiptoe into things. It is convenient to hedge my bets. By compartmentalizing and under committing, I can protect my investment and my pride.

I suppose there may be some value in not jumping all the way into things in some areas of life. Unfortunately, we bring this idea into our faith too often. We segment our faith so that it does not intrude into the rest of our life. If it threatens to inconvenience us, we can raise the gates to protect the rest of our lives.

God is looking for total commitment in people. He is recruiting those who would devote their whole heart, whole soul, and whole strength. In effect, he seeks those who would hold nothing back from their love for Him.

What do you hold back? How have you been hedging your bets? Are you willing to offer everything to the LORD this year? Will you love God in an unrestrained manner, giving all to Him?

REFLECT

What areas of your life do you hold back from God?

Do you fear giving everything to God? Why?

Do you want to love the LORD with all your heart, soul, and strength this year? If so, are you willing to make the necessary sacrifices to pursue this?

What rhythms can you put in place to chase after it?

MY WEEKLY GOALS

Jot down goals & activities for the week.

Love God

This week I will love God by:

☐

☐

☐

☐

☐

Love Neighbor

This week I will love my neighbors by:

☐

☐

☐

☐

☐

PRAISE & PRAYERS

Daily Prayers
Each morning and evening pray the daily prayers.

Praise
God, this week I praise you for:

☐

☐

☐

Personal Prayers
God, please move in these areas of my life this week:

☐

☐

☐

Prayers for Others
God, this week please move in the following neighbors lives:

☐

☐

☐

JOURNAL

AS YOURSELF

Date: _____

VERSE OF THE WEEK

You shall not take vengeance or bear a grudge against any of your people, but you shall love your neighbor as yourself: I am the Lord.

LEVITICUS 19:18

READING PLAN

- ☐ Luke 3:23-4:13
- ☐ Luke 4:14-44
- ☐ Luke 5:1-39
- ☐ Luke 6:1-49
- ☐ Luke 7:1-35
- ☐ Luke 7:36-8:3
- ☐ Psalm 3
- ☐ Psalm 4
- ☐ Psalm 5

DEVOTIONAL THOUGHT

Read Leviticus 19:9-18

Imagine someone on a deserted island, waiting to be rescued. She wonders if help will arrive. Do you ever contemplate if there are people around you that are waiting for someone to show them the love of Jesus? What if you are the one that carries the hope they are waiting for?

Many in this world are disillusioned by the way humans treat one another. Many are at their wit's end. Many are looking for someone who will love them the way they love themselves.

Loving a neighbor as yourself is not a one-time decision. It is a moment-by-moment choice to reflect the love of Jesus and care for others. It is a continual decision to humbly value others to such a degree that you will treat them in a manner worthy of a child of God.

Over the next 12 months, will you commit to daily starting fresh and resolving to love your neighbor as yourself - regardless of the circumstances, regardless of what they have done to you, regardless of whether they seem to deserve it?

REFLECT

Which neighbors is God calling you to love this year?

What are some ways you can learn more about their stories?

List some ways that you might tangibly love your neighbor as yourself this year. Look at the *Ideas for Loving Neighbors* section if you need inspiration.

What excuses are likely to prevent you from following through on these actions? How can you ensure that you will carry these out?

MY WEEKLY GOALS

Jot down goals & activities for the week.

Love God

This week I will love God by:

☐

☐

☐

☐

☐

Love Neighbor

This week I will love my neighbors by:

☐

☐

☐

☐

☐

PRAISE & PRAYERS

Daily Prayers
Each morning and evening pray the daily prayers.

Praise
God, this week I praise you for:

☐

☐

☐

Personal Prayers
God, please move in these areas of my life this week:

☐

☐

☐

Prayers for Others
God, this week please move in the following neighbors lives:

☐

☐

☐

JOURNAL

ADMIRING GOD'S GLORY

Date: _____

VERSE OF THE WEEK

Praise the Lord! Praise God in his sanctuary; praise him in his mighty firmament! Praise him for his mighty deeds; praise him according to his surpassing greatness!

PSALM 150:1-2

READING PLAN

- [ ] Luke 8:4-21
- [ ] Luke 8:22-56
- [ ] Luke 9:1-50
- [ ] Luke 9:51-10:24
- [ ] Luke 10:25-42
- [ ] Luke 11:1-36
- [ ] Psalm 6
- [ ] Psalm 7
- [ ] Psalm 8

DEVOTIONAL THOUGHT

Read Psalm 150

Our gaze lingers on a beautiful sunset. We scream at the top of our lungs at sports games. We fawn over rock stars and celebrities. Does the Almighty God not deserve that and much more?

We serve a God who created the universe and sustains it. A God whose majesty reaches beyond the limits of our comprehension. A God who made the deepest sacrifice to restore His relationship with you. A God who is working to redeem all things.

This is not just *a god*. He is the *God*. He is the LORD. He is Jesus Christ.

Open your eyes to see His grandeur. Ponder His glory. Marvel at His feats. Sing and shout His praise from the rooftops.

REFLECT

List some places where you best recognize God's glory. How do these reveal the Creator to you?

When was the last time you paused to reflect on God's glory? Will you make time to do so this week? Make a plan.

How can you glorify God with your actions this week?

Where are you seeing God move this week?

MY WEEKLY GOALS
Jot down goals & activities for the week.

Love God
This week I will love God by:

☐

☐

☐

☐

☐

Love Neighbor
This week I will love my neighbors by:

☐

☐

☐

☐

☐

PRAISE & PRAYERS

Daily Prayers
Each morning and evening pray the daily prayers.

Praise
God, this week I praise you for:

☐

☐

☐

Personal Prayers
God, please move in these areas of my life this week:

☐

☐

☐

Prayers for Others
God, this week please move in the following neighbors lives:

☐

☐

☐

JOURNAL

AGENTS OF HOPE

Date: _____

VERSE OF THE WEEK

So we are ambassadors for Christ, since God is making his appeal through us; we entreat you on behalf of Christ, be reconciled to God.

2 CORINTHIANS 5:20

READING PLAN

- ☐ Luke 11:37-12:12
- ☐ Luke 12:13-13:9
- ☐ Luke 13:10-35
- ☐ Luke 14
- ☐ Luke 15
- ☐ Psalm 9
- ☐ Psalm 10
- ☐ Psalm 11

DEVOTIONAL THOUGHT

Read 2 Corinthians 5:11-21

I really liked spy movies growing up. The adventure of it all was thrilling. I really enjoyed the clandestine actions, the gadgets and technology, and the excitement of the climactic moments. But there was something more to it than that. I was so impressed by the commitment of the operatives. They gave up their lives and risked their well-being for the sake of the cause. These were not just ordinary citizens going through the motions. These were agents of the cause.

God, too, is looking for agents. He does not seek secret agents who fight for earthly power but operatives who deliver the message of reconciliation to the world. He calls those who have received grace to be ambassadors of grace. He sends them out on a mission: to bring hope to the world.

You have been recruited into the mission of God's Kingdom. The mission is to share the hope, grace, and reconciliation that are in the process of transforming you to those who need Good News. Will you choose to accept it?

REFLECT

Do you see yourself as an agent of hope, commissioned to bring God's message of reconciliation to the world? Why or why not?

What are you afraid to risk for the mission of bringing the message of reconiliation to the world?

What is one concrete action you can take this week to respond to God's call on your life?

Who is God calling you to bring His message of hope, grace, and reconciliation to this week?

MY WEEKLY GOALS

Jot down goals & activities for the week.

Love God
This week I will love God by:

☐

☐

☐

☐

☐

Love Neighbor
This week I will love my neighbors by:

☐

☐

☐

☐

☐

PRAISE & PRAYERS

Daily Prayers

Each morning and evening pray the daily prayers.

Praise

God, this week I praise you for:

☐

☐

☐

Personal Prayers

God, please move in these areas of my life this week:

☐

☐

☐

Prayers for Others

God, this week please move in the following neighbors lives:

☐

☐

☐

JOURNAL

FOR WHO HE IS

Date: _____

VERSE OF THE WEEK

I will extol you, my God and King, and bless your name forever and ever. Every day I will bless you, and praise your name forever and ever. Great is the Lord, and greatly to be praised; his greatness is unsearchable.

PSALM 145:1-3

READING PLAN

- ☐ Luke 16:1-17:10
- ☐ Luke 17:11-37
- ☐ Luke 18:1-30
- ☐ Luke 18:31-19:27
- ☐ Luke 19:28-46
- ☐ Luke 19:47-20:44
- ☐ Psalm 12
- ☐ Psalm 13
- ☐ Psalm 14

DEVOTIONAL THOUGHT

Read Psalm 145

In the fast-paced world we live in, we often judge ourselves and others based on accomplishments. The more recently someone has demonstrated their greatness or affection for us, the easier it can be to celebrate them. What can get lost in the mix, however, is the idea that a person can have value outside of what they do.

We often place the same principle onto God. It is straightforward to praise God when He has just saved us, healed us, blessed us, or otherwise demonstrated His power to us. But the Almighty God is worthy of love and praise for who He is outside of what He has done.

Our God is loving, majestic, just, merciful, gracious, creative, powerful, compassionate, mighty, faithful, and so much more. He is worthy of praise for who He is. Spend some time reflecting on the goodness and splendor of the LORD this week. Love and appreciate Him for who He is.

REFLECT

List three characteristics of God that you particularly celebrate.

Why did you choose those characteristics? What do they mean to you?

How might you emulate these traits this week?

How might others be impacted if you reflect these characteristics of God you celebrate to them?

MY WEEKLY GOALS

Jot down goals & activities for the week.

Love God

This week I will love God by:

☐

☐

☐

☐

☐

Love Neighbor

This week I will love my neighbors by:

☐

☐

☐

☐

☐

PRAISE & PRAYERS

Daily Prayers

Each morning and evening pray the daily prayers.

Praise

God, this week I praise you for:

☐

☐

☐

Personal Prayers

God, please move in these areas of my life this week:

☐

☐

☐

Prayers for Others

God, this week please move in the following neighbors lives:

☐

☐

☐

JOURNAL

HUMBLE LOVE

Date: _____

VERSE OF THE WEEK

Do nothing from selfish ambition or conceit, but in humility regard others as better than yourselves.

PHILIPPIANS 2:3

READING PLAN

- ☐ Luke 20:45-21:38
- ☐ Luke 22:1-46
- ☐ Luke 22:47-23:25
- ☐ Luke 23:26-56
- ☐ Luke 24
- ☐ Acts 1
- ☐ Psalm 15
- ☐ Psalm 16
- ☐ Psalm 17

DEVOTIONAL THOUGHT

Read Philippians 2:1-11

"Regard others as better than yourselves." Wow! That is hard! Is it not? Maybe as equals. Maybe. But "better"? Is there not a translation issue here to provide me with an escape?

In a world where we are constantly trying to prove our worth, demonstrate that we belong, and gain the approval of others; this is not ingrained in us. But Jesus Himself models this for us in His grand act of leaving the comfort of heaven and emptying Himself to sacrifice Himself for people on earth. Now, this is not a call to self-deprecation. It is not a command to disparage your own value. You are created in the image of God and are full of purpose and value. Instead, this is a call to recognize the worth of others. To regard others as better than yourself is to see them as God sees them and to join Him in His grand rescue mission.

Do you find this challenging? Reflect on why this is hard for you. Do the challenging, self-examining work to break down the reasons why this may be the case. Pray that you might have humility and love for others to such a degree that there is nothing that would hold you back from looking out for the interests of others.

REFLECT

Do you consider yourself to be humble? In what ways?

Where and why do you struggle with humility?

Reflect on a time when someone valued your needs above their own. How did that impact you?

Think of one area where you struggle to put others' interests above your own. How might this look different if you walked with the same mind as Jesus?

MY WEEKLY GOALS

Jot down goals & activities for the week.

Love God

This week I will love God by:

☐

☐

☐

☐

☐

Love Neighbor

This week I will love my neighbors by:

☐

☐

☐

☐

☐

PRAISE & PRAYERS

Daily Prayers
Each morning and evening pray the daily prayers.

Praise
God, this week I praise you for:

☐

☐

☐

Personal Prayers
God, please move in these areas of my life this week:

☐

☐

☐

Prayers for Others
God, this week please move in the following neighbors lives:

☐

☐

☐

JOURNAL

FOR WHAT HE HAS DONE

Date: _____

VERSE OF THE WEEK

O give thanks to the Lord of lords, for his steadfast love endures forever; who alone does great wonders, for his steadfast love endures forever; who by understanding made the heavens, for his steadfast love endures forever; who spread out the earth on the waters, for his steadfast love endures forever.

PSALM 136:3-6

READING PLAN

- ☐ Acts 2
- ☐ Acts 3:1-4:31
- ☐ Acts 4:32-6:7
- ☐ Acts 6:8-7:60
- ☐ Acts 8
- ☐ Acts 9:1-31
- ☐ Psalm 18
- ☐ Psalm 19
- ☐ Psalm 20

DEVOTIONAL THOUGHT

Read Psalm 136

Once might be random. Twice might be a coincidence. Three times might be luck. But a continual, repeated event is a pattern. It is something that we can count on; something that we can trust.

In our world, this can be hard to find. Rules are broken. People fall short. It is said that the only thing that is constant is change. However, the LORD has a track record of demonstrated actions to care for and protect His people. He has repeatedly rescued, blessed, healed, restored, provided, comforted, forgiven, and saved humans.

In fact, in the Old Testament God was perhaps most well-known for steadfast love - better translated as covenant faithfulness. The people knew that God, who had shown up so many times before, would surely come to their aid again. They knew that He would hold up His end of the pact. It was clear that

He was committed to His people.

A couple of weeks ago we focused on praising God for who He is. Now we turn to what He has done. Celebrate His great deeds! Appreciate His gracious acts. Praise His name for all He has done, continues to do, and even those things you can count on Him to do into the future.

REFLECT

What is one pivotal act you have seen God perform in your life? Praise Him for that this week.

List a few of the most important things God has done throughout history. Celebrate them.

Write a thank you letter to the Lord. Praise Him for all the incredible things He has done. Store the letter so that you might return to it in times of trial.

Is there someone in your life that needs hope this week? Encourage them by sharing how God has shown up in the past and how He offers hope for a restored future.

MY WEEKLY GOALS

Jot down goals & activities for the week.

Love God

This week I will love God by:

☐

☐

☐

☐

☐

Love Neighbor

This week I will love my neighbors by:

☐

☐

☐

☐

☐

PRAISE & PRAYERS

Daily Prayers
Each morning and evening pray the daily prayers.

Praise
God, this week I praise you for:

☐

☐

☐

Personal Prayers
God, please move in these areas of my life this week:

☐

☐

☐

Prayers for Others
God, this week please move in the following neighbors lives:

☐

☐

☐

JOURNAL

SEE THE UNSEEN

Date: _____

VERSE OF THE WEEK

For I was hungry and you gave me food, I was thirsty and you gave me something to drink, I was a stranger and you welcomed me, I was naked and you gave me clothing, I was sick and you took care of me, I was in prison and you visited me.

MATTHEW 25:35-36

READING PLAN

- ☐ Acts 9:32-43
- ☐ Acts 10:1-11:18
- ☐ Acts 11:19-30
- ☐ Acts 12
- ☐ Acts 13-14
- ☐ Acts 15:1-35
- ☐ Acts 15:36-17:15
- ☐ Psalm 21
- ☐ Psalm 22
- ☐ Psalm 23

DEVOTIONAL THOUGHT

Read Matthew 25:31-46

How many of those lane reflectors did you see on the last street you drove down? Can you list all the plants you saw yesterday? How many advertisements have you seen online and on television this week?

Our brains are trained to filter out seemingly irrelevant, ambient noise. We focus on those things that seem important and exclude those that do not. Unfortunately, we apply the same principle to humans and oftentimes filter out people that are in need. This especially happens with the hungry, the imprisoned, the sick, the foreigner, and the needy. Whether they come into our line of sight or not, they can go unseen.

As people called to care for the sick and hurting, serve the most vulnerable in society, and seek the lost, we should seek out and help those in need. We should retrain our eyes to see those that have been written off, despised, and forgotten. We should show them the love that God showed us.

Jesus says that "*just as you did it to one of the least of these who are members of my family, you did it to me.*" Are you seeing and responding to the least of these? Or are you ignoring Jesus? How might your week be different if you treated every last person you encountered as if you were interacting with Jesus Himself? How might you do that this week?

REFLECT

Contemplate those that you fail to notice or even consider unworthy of love and care?

Do you ever consider that you are interacting with Jesus when you deal with others? How might that influence your interactions?

How might you change your worldview so that you would see those in need?

Will you determine to treat them as if they were Jesus?

MY WEEKLY GOALS

Jot down goals & activities for the week.

Love God

This week I will love God by:

☐

☐

☐

☐

☐

Love Neighbor

This week I will love my neighbors by:

☐

☐

☐

☐

☐

PRAISE & PRAYERS

Daily Prayers

Each morning and evening pray the daily prayers.

Praise

God, this week I praise you for:

☐

☐

☐

Personal Prayers

God, please move in these areas of my life this week:

☐

☐

☐

Prayers for Others

God, this week please move in the following neighbors lives:

☐

☐

☐

JOURNAL

SEEK THE LORD

Date: _____

VERSE OF THE WEEK

When you search for me, you will find me; if you seek me with all your heart, I will let you find me, says the Lord, and I will restore your fortunes and gather you from all the nations and all the places where I have driven you, says the Lord, and I will bring you back to the place from which I sent you into exile.

JEREMIAH 29:13-14

READING PLAN

☐ Acts 17:16-34   ☐ Acts 19:23-20:16   ☐ Psalm 24
☐ Acts 18:1-22   ☐ Acts 20:17-21:16   ☐ Psalm 25
☐ Acts 18:23-19:22   ☐ Acts 21:17-23:11   ☐ Psalm 26

DEVOTIONAL THOUGHT

Read Jeremiah 29:10-14

I remember that I once walked into a room to discover one of my kids hiding behind a curtain. He was playing hide-and-seek. I had actually won without even knowing I was playing, let alone searching for him. This was the anomaly though. If you want to win at that game, you have to seek out those that are covertly hiding in order to avoid detection. And so it is with many things in life. We have to look for them or pursue them. Rarely do things fall into our lap.

Sometimes we expect God to show up in our lives with fanfare and gift boxes - even before we invite Him in. And while God may unexpectedly interrupt the lives of those that are not all looking for Him at times, He often reveals Himself to those who seek Him out.

Do you actively search for the LORD? Do you invite His presence into your life? Do you chase after

Him with all your heart?

Seek out and invite God to move in your life this week. Ask and expect Him to show up. Don't just ask once and wait passively. Seek Him. Look for Him. Search for Him. And see what happens when you diligently pursue Him.

REFLECT

Do you actively search for the Lord? Or do you passively wait for Him to show up?

Do you believe that God will respond if you seek Him with all your heart? Do you believe that God loves you enough to respond to you? Why or why not?

What is one way that you could diligently pursue God this week?

MY WEEKLY GOALS

Jot down goals & activities for the week.

Love God

This week I will love God by:

☐

☐

☐

☐

☐

Love Neighbor

This week I will love my neighbors by:

☐

☐

☐

☐

☐

PRAISE & PRAYERS

Daily Prayers

Each morning and evening pray the daily prayers.

Praise

God, this week I praise you for:

☐

☐

☐

Personal Prayers

God, please move in these areas of my life this week:

☐

☐

☐

Prayers for Others

God, this week please move in the following neighbors lives:

☐

☐

☐

JOURNAL

SERVING ONE ANOTHER

Date: _____

VERSE OF THE WEEK

Like good stewards of the manifold grace of God, serve one another with whatever gift each of you has received.

1 PETER 4:10

READING PLAN

☐ Acts 23:12-24:27   ☐ Romans 1:1-17   ☐ Psalm 28
☐ Acts 25-26   ☐ Romans 1:18-32   ☐ Psalm 29
☐ Acts 27:1-28:15   ☐ Romans 2:1-16
☐ Acts 28:16-31   ☐ Psalm 27

DEVOTIONAL THOUGHT

Read 1 Peter 4:7-11

The way of the world generally works in a manner where you gain wealth for your personal use. While there is a capitalistic concept of wealth creation, scarcity drives much of our action. The more you have, the less there is for me. The economy of God operates differently. There is abundance as the Creator God is intimately involved with His people. Moreover, what we have been blessed with is intended to be a blessing to those around us - not merely for our own stockpiling and consumption.

We are called to steward the gifts of God. This does not mean that we are to hide and protect our gifts. Rather, we are called to put our gifts into action in order to bless the world. Stewardship, then, is not merely preservation. Stewardship is putting the gifts of God into effect in useful ways that build others up and align with God's Kingdom purposes.

What has God blessed you with that you have been withholding in part or in whole? What has been holding you back from giving your gifts and assets away? Is it fear, greed, apathy? If you were to remove these hindrances, what might God accomplish through you?

REFLECT

Do you consider the time, talents and treasures that are at your disposal to be yours or resources that you steward for God?

Consider what hinders you from leveraging your resources to serve one another. Are you too busy? Too selfish? Too distracted? Something else?

Reflect on what God has previously accomplished through you when you offered yourself to His service.

Are you aware of any opportunities to serve others this week? If the opportunity arises (whether planned or spontaneous), will you choose to love others?

MY WEEKLY GOALS

Jot down goals & activities for the week.

Love God

This week I will love God by:

☐

☐

☐

☐

☐

Love Neighbor

This week I will love my neighbors by:

☐

☐

☐

☐

☐

PRAISE & PRAYERS

Daily Prayers
Each morning and evening pray the daily prayers.

Praise
God, this week I praise you for:

☐

☐

☐

Personal Prayers
God, please move in these areas of my life this week:

☐

☐

☐

Prayers for Others
God, this week please move in the following neighbors lives:

☐

☐

☐

JOURNAL

TRUST IN THE LORD

Date: _____

VERSE OF THE WEEK

Let me hear of your steadfast love in the morning, for in you I put my trust. Teach me the way I should go, for to you I lift up my soul.

PSALM 143:8

READING PLAN

☐ Romans 2:17-3:8	☐ Romans 4	☐ Psalm 30
☐ Romans 3:9-20	☐ Romans 5:1-11	☐ Psalm 31
☐ Romans 3:21-31	☐ Romans 5:12-21	☐ Psalm 32

DEVOTIONAL THOUGHT

Read Psalm 143

Some of the most dangerous words uttered throughout history may be, "*do you trust me?*" Trust makes us vulnerable. Trust puts us at the mercy of another. Trust relinquishes control. Oh, how I have a hard time with that one!

Do you trust God with your health? With provision for your needs? With direction for your steps? Of course, it is easy to say that we trust God. It is harder to live it out. It is easy to say that we trust God. It is harder to stay faithful when the road is dark. It is easy to say that we trust God. It is harder to maintain trust when His plans look different than ours.

Do you trust that His ways lead to blessing, goodness, and wholeness? Do you trust that His path for your life is worth pursuing and will be of eternal value? Will you?

May you trust in the Lord. May you trust in His plans and purposes. May the prayer of your heart be:

"Your Kingdom come. Your will be done."

REFLECT

Do you have a hard time trusting people? What about trusting God?

Why do you find it difficult to trust?

What are some of the most challenging areas of your life to trust God with?

Write down some of the ways that God has showed up in the past. Pray that you might trust Him to move in these current challenges as well.

MY WEEKLY GOALS

Jot down goals & activities for the week.

Love God

This week I will love God by:

☐

☐

☐

☐

☐

Love Neighbor

This week I will love my neighbors by:

☐

☐

☐

☐

☐

PRAISE & PRAYERS

Daily Prayers

Each morning and evening pray the daily prayers.

Praise

God, this week I praise you for:

☐

☐

☐

Personal Prayers

God, please move in these areas of my life this week:

☐

☐

☐

Prayers for Others

God, this week please move in the following neighbors lives:

☐

☐

☐

JOURNAL

DEMONSTRATION OF MERCY

Date: _____

VERSE OF THE WEEK

Which of these three, do you think, was a neighbor to the man who fell into the hands of the robbers?" He said, "The one who showed him mercy." Jesus said to him, "Go and do likewise."

LUKE 10:36-37

READING PLAN

☐ Romans 6	☐ Romans 8:18-39	☐ Psalm 33
☐ Romans 7	☐ Romans 9:1-29	☐ Psalm 34
☐ Romans 8:1-17	☐ Romans 9:30-10:21	☐ Psalm 35

DEVOTIONAL THOUGHT

Read Luke 10:25-37

We, humans, tend to ask, "*Who is my neighbor?*" However, Jesus answers a different question altogether. He turns it back on us and asks us how we can be a neighbor to those we encounter. There is a critical difference between knowing our neighbors and living like a neighbor.

If we could easily define who our neighbors are, we could limit our responsibility and liability. Loving our neighbors, on the other hand, comes down to acting like a neighbor to those in need. It involves getting our hands dirty. It involves doing the things that most do not want to do. It involves sacrificing our own finances and well-being for the benefit of those we encounter. It involves allowing our heart to take over as opposed to adhering to a set of predetermined practices. It involves showing mercy. It involves doing for those we encounter just as God would do for us, holding nothing back.

Do you try to limit how and who you will help? Do you eagerly come to the aid of all those in need or do you contrive rationalizations as to why they do not need help or why you are unable to help? Are you willing to get your hands dirty - literally or metaphorically - for the Kingdom's cause?

This week, open your heart to address the messy needs of those you might encounter. Root out those desires to justify why someone is not your neighbor, why they are undeserving, or why you are unavailable. Stop asking how you can limit your obligation and start asking how you can become a mercy-showing neighbor to all you encounter.

REFLECT

Ask yourself honestly: do you typically help those in need?

Do you make excuses to avoid assisting those you dislike or consider undeserving?

Who are some of the neighbors you are surrounded with?

List out those you have a harder time showing mercy to. Pray that your heart towards them might change.

MY WEEKLY GOALS

Jot down goals & activities for the week.

Love God

This week I will love God by:

☐

☐

☐

☐

☐

Love Neighbor

This week I will love my neighbors by:

☐

☐

☐

☐

☐

PRAISE & PRAYERS

Daily Prayers

Each morning and evening pray the daily prayers.

Praise

God, this week I praise you for:

☐

☐

☐

Personal Prayers

God, please move in these areas of my life this week:

☐

☐

☐

Prayers for Others

God, this week please move in the following neighbors lives:

☐

☐

☐

JOURNAL

GRASPING HIS LOVE FOR US

Date: _____

VERSE OF THE WEEK

For God so loved the world that he gave his only Son, so that everyone who believes in him may not perish but may have eternal life.

JOHN 3:16

READING PLAN

☐ Romans 11	☐ Romans 14	☐ Psalm 36
☐ Romans 12	☐ Romans 15:1-13	☐ Psalm 37
☐ Romans 13	☐ Romans 15:14-33	☐ Psalm 38

DEVOTIONAL THOUGHT

Read John 3:1-21

If I'm honest, at times I have struggled to believe or understand that someone could love me. As we struggle to believe that we can be loved, it can be hard to love in return. Similarly, if we struggle to believe why or how God could love us, it can be hard to love Him in return.

"*Jesus loves you*" is not just a catchy saying. Jesus' love for all people and for you specifically is so powerful that it motivates Him to pursue you at even the greatest cost. In you, He sees someone created in His image, who has incredible worth and value, and who He knows intimately. He loves you so incredibly much that the thought of not being in a relationship with you seemed unbearable. His love drove Him to change the course of history by sending and sacrificing His own Son.

Think about that. Even in your darkest moment, even considering your most horrific thought or action, even when you didn't believe you yourself were deserving of love, God valued your life. He forgives those things you think unforgivable. He sees value where you may not. He loves you no mat-

115

ter what. That is not just a saying. It is a reality.

Reflect on His love for you this week.

REFLECT

Do you feel deserving of love? Why or why not?

Whether deserved or not, can you comprehend that the Lord loves you deeply?

Do you find it hard to believe that the Almighty God could love you?

Write down that God deeply loves you. Write it again and again. Read it out loud and let it sink in this week. You are loved!

MY WEEKLY GOALS

Jot down goals & activities for the week.

Love God

This week I will love God by:

☐

☐

☐

☐

☐

Love Neighbor

This week I will love my neighbors by:

☐

☐

☐

☐

☐

PRAISE & PRAYERS

Daily Prayers

Each morning and evening pray the daily prayers.

Praise

God, this week I praise you for:

- ☐

- ☐

- ☐

Personal Prayers

God, please move in these areas of my life this week:

- ☐

- ☐

- ☐

Prayers for Others

God, this week please move in the following neighbors lives:

- ☐

- ☐

- ☐

JOURNAL

SIMPLY LOVE

Date: _____

VERSE OF THE WEEK

For the whole law is summed up in a single commandment, "You shall love your neighbor as yourself."

GALATIANS 5:14

READING PLAN

- ☐ Romans 16
- ☐ 1 Corinthians 1:1-17
- ☐ 1 Corinthians 1:18-31
- ☐ 1 Corinthians 2
- ☐ 1 Corinthians 3
- ☐ 1 Corinthians 4
- ☐ 1 Corinthians 5
- ☐ Psalm 39
- ☐ Psalm 40
- ☐ Psalm 41

DEVOTIONAL THOUGHT

Read Galatians 5:13-15

Have you ever heard of the concept of "*paralysis by analysis*"? It is the idea that we can overanalyze things to such a degree that it leads to inaction. Oftentimes, we can become overwhelmed by a myriad of options or by trying to find the perfect path forward that we become paralyzed.

Faith is not exempt from this idea. Do these things. Don't do those. Learn this. Don't look like that. Follow this list. Avoid the things on that list. And on and on for thousands upon thousands of verses. The whole thing can feel very complicated - which can produce inaction.

But the essence of our Christian faith is really simple: love God and love neighbor. All of the dos and don'ts, all of the laws, all of the commandments about human interactions can be summed up in the idea of loving those that were created in the image of God.

Don't wait for the most strategic plan. Don't wait for the most serendipitous moment. Don't wait for perfection in your own life. Love your neighbor this week in even the simplest of ways. Even a smile, a hug, a generous gift, an attentive listening, an empathetic act, or a selfless decision can catalyze transformation both in you and in your neighbor.

REFLECT

Do you ever feel overwhelmed with your faith?

Do you feel like the complexity makes you stagnant? Or do you respond differently?

Do you find the simplicity of the "law" reassuring?

What is one, achievable action you can take this week? Make a plan to do it. Maybe even calendar it. Allow this to ignite you and get things moving.

MY WEEKLY GOALS

Jot down goals & activities for the week.

Love God
This week I will love God by:

☐

☐

☐

☐

☐

Love Neighbor
This week I will love my neighbors by:

☐

☐

☐

☐

☐

PRAISE & PRAYERS

Daily Prayers

Each morning and evening pray the daily prayers.

Praise

God, this week I praise you for:

☐

☐

☐

Personal Prayers

God, please move in these areas of my life this week:

☐

☐

☐

Prayers for Others

God, this week please move in the following neighbors lives:

☐

☐

☐

JOURNAL

REST IN HIM

Date: _____

VERSE OF THE WEEK

I will both lie down and sleep in peace;
for you alone, O Lord, make me lie down in safety.

Psalm 4:8

READING PLAN

☐ 1 Corinthians 6	☐ 1 Corinthians 9	☐ Psalm 42
☐ 1 Corinthians 7	☐ 1 Corinthians 10:1-11:1	☐ Psalm 43
☐ 1 Corinthians 8	☐ 1 Corinthians 11:2-34	☐ Psalm 44

DEVOTIONAL THOUGHT

Read Psalm 4

Exercise. Breakfast. Work. Lunch. More work. Store. Home. Family. Dinner. Events. Chores. And repeat. Life races so quickly that it can feel as if we hardly have time to catch our breath. Throw a little stress and worry into the mix and true rest can be elusive.

Too many of us - myself included - wear our busyness as a badge of honor and importance. Yet, a frenzied life can be a challenge for both health and faith.

Pause.... Take a deep breath.... Now, take another.

Remember that the LORD sustains and protects. He has neither forgotten nor forsaken you. Moreover, He loves you regardless of what you do this week. No need to earn that love. He offers you rest and peace.

Pause again… Breathe in... Breathe out... Breathe in the words *"Lord Jesus Christ, Son of the Living God"*.... Breathe out the words *"Have mercy on me a sinner"*... Slowly and peacefully repeat.

Rest in His loving, merciful embrace this week.

REFLECT

Do you feel like the world spins too fast? Do you feel like you are so busy that you cannot find time for important areas of your life - like your faith? Reflect on the impact this has on you.

How do you protect against busyness?

What do you prioritize when there is a lot going on in your life?

Where in your schedule can to make time to stop and rest in the Lord? The busier you are the more important it is to take time. If you feel like this is impossible, start with just a few minutes. During this time be sure to breathe deeply and tune out all distrations. Know that God loves you. As you rest in His arms, quietly thank Him for caring for you.

MY WEEKLY GOALS

Jot down goals & activities for the week.

Love God

This week I will love God by:

☐

☐

☐

☐

☐

Love Neighbor

This week I will love my neighbors by:

☐

☐

☐

☐

☐

PRAISE & PRAYERS

Daily Prayers
Each morning and evening pray the daily prayers.

Praise
God, this week I praise you for:

☐

☐

☐

Personal Prayers
God, please move in these areas of my life this week:

☐

☐

☐

Prayers for Others
God, this week please move in the following neighbors lives:

☐

☐

☐

JOURNAL

BECAUSE GOD'S LOVE IS IN US

Date: _____

VERSE OF THE WEEK

Beloved, let us love one another, because love is from God; everyone who loves is born of God and knows God. Whoever does not love does not know God, for God is love.

1 JOHN 4:7-8

READING PLAN

☐ 1 Corinthians 12	☐ 1 Corinthians 16	☐ Psalm 46
☐ 1 Corinthians 13	☐ 2 Corinthians 1:1-11	☐ Psalm 47
☐ 1 Corinthians 14	☐ 2 Corinthians 1:12-2:11	
☐ 1 Corinthians 15	☐ Psalm 45	

DEVOTIONAL THOUGHT

Read 1 John 4:7-21

Have you ever over zealously deluged your meal with salt while cooking? When that happens, it seems that no matter what you do, you cannot mask it. It desperately wants to burst through.

The same could be said of God's love. If God's love is indeed found in us, there is no preventing it from shining through. We cannot help but love our neighbors because there is no stopping the love of God inside of us. We might try to contain it. We might resist it through selfish actions. But, if the love of God resides in us, we will love one another.

If you claim to love the Lord, then lean into His love and allow it to flow freely through you. If you love God's children, then you will know that you have been born of God.

Try to see others with the eyes of Jesus this week. Intentionally open up your heart that God's love might surge through you.

REFLECT

Do you feel generally feel capable of loving others? Why do you think that is?

In what areas do you most struggle with loving others?

Do you consider your efforts to love others an internal battle that you have to overcome on your own?

Do you believe that God's love is in you? If you desire to model His love, consider how you might allow Him to flow through you.

MY WEEKLY GOALS

Jot down goals & activities for the week.

Love God

This week I will love God by:

☐

☐

☐

☐

☐

Love Neighbor

This week I will love my neighbors by:

☐

☐

☐

☐

☐

PRAISE & PRAYERS

Daily Prayers

Each morning and evening pray the daily prayers.

Praise

God, this week I praise you for:

☐

☐

☐

Personal Prayers

God, please move in these areas of my life this week:

☐

☐

☐

Prayers for Others

God, this week please move in the following neighbors lives:

☐

☐

☐

JOURNAL

SET YOUR MIND ON HIM

Date: _____

VERSE OF THE WEEK

So if you have been raised with Christ, seek the things that are above, where Christ is, seated at the right hand of God. Set your minds on things that are above, not on things that are on earth, for you have died, and your life is hidden with Christ in God.

COLOSSIANS 3:1-3

READING PLAN

- ☐ 2 Corinthians 2:12-3:18
- ☐ 2 Corinthians 4:1-5:10
- ☐ 2 Corinthians 5:11-6:10
- ☐ 2 Corinthians 6:11-7:16
- ☐ 2 Corinthians 8-9
- ☐ 2 Corinthians 10:1-12
- ☐ Psalm 48
- ☐ Psalm 49
- ☐ Psalm 50

DEVOTIONAL THOUGHT

Read Colossians 3:1-17

He went to the grocery store to pick up milk - an essential in his home. Caught up in the samples, the sales, and all the foods that promised pleasure and fulfillment, he came home with bags full of goodies but had forgotten the milk. The secondary thing was confused with the primary. He lost sight of the point of the outing.

In our time on earth, God has a purpose for each one of us. We have a mission on our way to our eternal destination. Unfortunately, we are far too often distracted by the things of this world that offer empty promises of satisfaction, gratification, and life. While there are many good things that we can enjoy along the journey, we must never lose sight of the things above.

Focus on the God who loves you and has a purpose for you. If something has pushed its way in front of these things, realign your priorities and focus on the King with whom you will spend eternity.

REFLECT

What most draws your attention in life? Review your schedule to see where you spend your time.

What distracts you from setting your mind on eternity?

What kind of impact do you notice when you walk with your eyes firmly fixed on Jesus?

How might you refocus on the greater purpose God has for you? Are there things in your life that you need to deprioritize or remove entirely? Consider how you might fix your attention on the purposes God has for you.

MY WEEKLY GOALS

Jot down goals & activities for the week.

Love God

This week I will love God by:

☐

☐

☐

☐

☐

Love Neighbor

This week I will love my neighbors by:

☐

☐

☐

☐

☐

PRAISE & PRAYERS

Daily Prayers
Each morning and evening pray the daily prayers.

Praise
God, this week I praise you for:

☐

☐

☐

Personal Prayers
God, please move in these areas of my life this week:

☐

☐

☐

Prayers for Others
God, this week please move in the following neighbors lives:

☐

☐

☐

JOURNAL

STANDING WITH

Date: _____

VERSE OF THE WEEK

A friend loves at all times, and kinsfolk are born to share adversity.

PROVERBS 17:17

READING PLAN

☐ 2 Corinthians 10:13-12:13	☐ Galatians 2	☐ Psalm 51
☐ 2 Corinthians 12:14-13:14	☐ Galatians 3	☐ Psalm 52
☐ Galatians 1	☐ Galatians 4	☐ Psalm 53

DEVOTIONAL THOUGHT

Read Proverbs 17

The winds of friendship and so-called brotherhood can change quickly. A wrong move, a false accusation, a tough loss, or a single wrong word can bring a relationship to ruin.

When life comes crashing down on us, we often find ourselves standing alone in the ruins. Whether we bring destruction upon ourselves or are attacked from the outside, trials can be the cruelest, loneliest times. These are the times we are most vulnerable, most desperate, most isolated, and most in need of a true neighbor.

After all others have left, a true neighbor remains at our side. Despite that all others have gone to sleep, a true neighbor continues to be at our side. Even though all others have abandoned, a true neighbor stands firm.

Who is lonely and in need of your help this week? How can you share the burdens of a friend, family member, or neighbor? How can you uplift and bring comfort?

REFLECT

Think back to a time when you were attacked or that the most important people seemingly abandoned you. How did that make you feel?

When might you have attacked or left someone else feeling stranded? Contemplate how you might have acted differently and what the impact might have been.

Think about someone that stood with you in your time of trial. Or if nobody did, ponder how powerful it would have been if someone had.

Consider any neighbors that might be experiencing adversity currently and how you might support them.

MY WEEKLY GOALS

Jot down goals & activities for the week.

Love God

This week I will love God by:

☐

☐

☐

☐

☐

Love Neighbor

This week I will love my neighbors by:

☐

☐

☐

☐

☐

PRAISE & PRAYERS

Daily Prayers
Each morning and evening pray the daily prayers.

Praise
God, this week I praise you for:

☐

☐

☐

Personal Prayers
God, please move in these areas of my life this week:

☐

☐

☐

Prayers for Others
God, this week please move in the following neighbors lives:

☐

☐

☐

JOURNAL

FOLLOW HIS COMMANDS

Date: _____

VERSE OF THE WEEK

Whoever says, "I have come to know him," but does not obey his commandments, is a liar, and in such a person the truth does not exist; but whoever obeys his word, truly in this person the love of God has reached perfection. By this we may be sure that we are in him: whoever says, "I abide in him," ought to walk just as he walked.

1 JOHN 2:4-6

READING PLAN

- ☐ Galatians 5
- ☐ Galatians 6
- ☐ Ephesians 1
- ☐ Ephesians 2
- ☐ Ephesians 3
- ☐ Ephesians 4:1-16
- ☐ Ephesians 4:17-32
- ☐ Psalm 54
- ☐ Psalm 55
- ☐ Psalm 56

DEVOTIONAL THOUGHT

Read 1 John 2:1-6

Faith does not seem exempt from the desire to have our cake and eat it too. We often want both the grace of God and the unencumbered freedom to live our lives according to our sinful desires.

If we truly love God, however, we should walk in His ways. This is not to shackle you to arbitrary rules but to align you with the Lord in the joint goal of seeing His kingdom come and His will be done on earth as it is in heaven. The commandments of the Lord exist to put conditions in place that the whole world might be blessed. Actions, then, that disobey His commandments bring curse and destruction. Disobedience resists God's goals. How then can we claim to love God if we oppose His kingdom?

163

First, we must decide if we are for or against God. From there, let us choose to be obedient to the Lord. May we see ever greater alignment between our will and that of the Father. If we find ourselves disobeying, let us start fresh and recommit to His ways.

REFLECT

Do you generally view the commands of God as a burden that stands in the way of your plans?

Which of God' ways are the most challenging for you to abide by? Which do you flat out ignore or disobey?

Do you consider yourself to be for or against the Lord? Do your actions support that?

Meditate on what changes you ought to make in your life to better align with the ways of the God you love.

MY WEEKLY GOALS

Jot down goals & activities for the week.

Love God

This week I will love God by:

☐

☐

☐

☐

☐

Love Neighbor

This week I will love my neighbors by:

☐

☐

☐

☐

☐

PRAISE & PRAYERS

Daily Prayers
Each morning and evening pray the daily prayers.

Praise
God, this week I praise you for:

☐

☐

☐

Personal Prayers
God, please move in these areas of my life this week:

☐

☐

☐

Prayers for Others
God, this week please move in the following neighbors lives:

☐

☐

☐

JOURNAL

ONLY THOSE THAT LOVE YOU

Date: _____

VERSE OF THE WEEK

But love your enemies, do good, and lend, expecting nothing in return. Your reward will be great, and you will be children of the Most High; for he is kind to the ungrateful and the wicked. Be merciful, just as your Father is merciful.

LUKE 6:35-36

READING PLAN

- [ ] Ephesians 5:1-21
- [ ] Ephesians 5:22-6:9
- [ ] Ephesians 6:10-24
- [ ] Philippians 1:1-26
- [ ] Philippians 1:27-2:11
- [ ] Philippians 2:12-30
- [ ] Psalm 57
- [ ] Psalm 58
- [ ] Psalm 59

DEVOTIONAL THOUGHT

Read Luke 6:27-36

It is relatively easy to love and show kindness to those that care for and do good to us. Perhaps it is even easier to hate and withhold goodness from those who hate us and would do harm to us. It feels so natural and justified. We simply write those people off and move on. Surely our enemies are not our neighbors, right? Surely their sentiments and actions towards us disqualify them from our call to love? It seems both logical and justified.

Yet that is not actually what we are expected to do. Jesus very clearly calls us to love our enemies. He would have us do good to those that would do us harm. He would have us lend to those who cannot or would not repay. While this might seem illogical in the earthly realm, this is the way of God's Kingdom. In fact, if love was withheld from enemies, none of us would have received God's love in the first place. Ouch!

Who are your enemies? Who do you have a hard time showing love to? Or who do you explicitly withhold love and good deeds from?

Stop justifying blessing others based on logic, good business sense, or past history. This week, consider how Jesus would have you act differently in these situations. Choose to love and show kindness to all - especially to those who hate you.

REFLECT

Who do you think of as an adversary or struggle to love? List them out (using shorthand if others might see your journal).

Have you withheld love from these people? How have you justified that? What would Jesus have you do instead?

Do you choose to show love even to those that seem unlovable? If so, for each person listed above write down the following: "God loves [person's name]". Then, write: "I choose to love [person's name]". Pray that God would transform you heart so that you might love them regardless of what they might have done or whether they seem to deserve it or not.

MY WEEKLY GOALS

Jot down goals & activities for the week.

Love God

This week I will love God by:

☐

☐

☐

☐

☐

Love Neighbor

This week I will love my neighbors by:

☐

☐

☐

☐

☐

PRAISE & PRAYERS

Daily Prayers
Each morning and evening pray the daily prayers.

Praise
God, this week I praise you for:

☐

☐

☐

Personal Prayers
God, please move in these areas of my life this week:

☐

☐

☐

Prayers for Others
God, this week please move in the following neighbors lives:

☐

☐

☐

JOURNAL

WRESTLE FOR IT

Date: _____

VERSE OF THE WEEK

Then he said, "Let me go, for the day is breaking." But Jacob said, "I will not let you go, unless you bless me."

GENESIS 32:26

READING PLAN

- [ ] Philippians 3:1-4:1
- [ ] Philippians 4:2-23
- [ ] Colossians 1:1-20
- [ ] Colossians 1:21-2:5
- [ ] Colossians 2:6-23
- [ ] Colossians 3:1-17
- [ ] Colossians 3:18-4:18
- [ ] Psalm 60
- [ ] Psalm 61
- [ ] Psalm 62

DEVOTIONAL THOUGHT

Read Genesis 32:22-32

Are you hungry for God's presence in your life? Are you really hungry? Are you starving for it? Do you desire it to such a degree that you would battle for it? Do you love God so much that you cannot imagine your life without His presence and blessing in it?

Prior to an anticipated altercation with his brother Esau, Jacob had an encounter with God where He wrestles with Him during the night. His persistence was so great that he would not let go without a blessing. While he had no chance of actually defeating the Almighty, his persistence and hunger were so great that he achieved his goal. He received the desired blessing he strived for.

How far would you go for your love for God and your desire for His blessing in your life? This week, fight for His presence. Ask. Plead. Beg. Wrestle. Persist. If you pursue the Lord diligently, He will not withhold His presence from you.

REFLECT

Do you desire God's presence and blessing in your life?

Where are you looking for Jesus to show up? List out some of the areas that you are desperate for Him to show up in.

Are you hungry enough to wrestle with God?

What rhythm can you implement into your life in order to persistently, relentlessly pursue God's presence and seek His blessing?

MY WEEKLY GOALS

Jot down goals & activities for the week.

Love God
This week I will love God by:

☐

☐

☐

☐

☐

Love Neighbor
This week I will love my neighbors by:

☐

☐

☐

☐

☐

PRAISE & PRAYERS

Daily Prayers
Each morning and evening pray the daily prayers.

Praise
God, this week I praise you for:

☐

☐

☐

Personal Prayers
God, please move in these areas of my life this week:

☐

☐

☐

Prayers for Others
God, this week please move in the following neighbors lives:

☐

☐

☐

JOURNAL

SINCERE LOVE

Date: _____

VERSE OF THE WEEK

Now that you have purified your souls by your obedience to the truth so that you have genuine mutual love, love one another deeply from the heart. You have been born anew, not of perishable but of imperishable seed, through the living and enduring word of God.

1 PETER 1:22-23

READING PLAN

☐ 1 Thessalonians 1	☐ 1 Thessalonians 4:1-12	☐ Psalm 63
☐ 1 Thessalonians 2:1-16	☐ 1 Thessalonians 4:13-5:11	☐ Psalm 64
☐ 1 Thessalonians 2:17-3:13	☐ 1 Thessalonians 5:12-22	☐ Psalm 65

DEVOTIONAL THOUGHT

Read 1 Peter 1:3-25

To be candid, sometimes my heart is not in things. If I'm even more honest, sometimes I feel indifferent about that. I kind of want someone to tell me what to do so that I can take care of it, move on, and get the requester to leave me alone.

This does not work with neighbor loving. The scriptures are filled with commands that tell us what to do. Even when clearly outlined, we can struggle. However, even if we were able to follow the prescribed actions without any alignment of the heart, it would fall far short of God's desire for how humans should interact. Anyone that has watched kids apologize to one another when instructed to do so knows how painful this can be.

God calls us to sincerely love our neighbors. No checklist, no command, and no forced actions can circumvent this. Loving others should come from the heart. If we look at the wholeness and restoration that will be experienced in eternity, then we understand why this is not only important but a demonstration of God's Kingdom here on earth. It is not about an empty act but about a reconciled people living in harmony.

This is far from easy, however - especially as we remember that we are called to love our enemies. This week pray that the Holy Spirit would transform your heart. Ask that He would fill you with true or agape love for neighbors. Petition that God would let you see your neighbors as He sees them. Ask, seek, and knock at God's door until your heart starts changing. Then keep asking.

REFLECT

Be honest. Do you authentically love others?

Where do you love most sincerely?

Where are you insincere in your love?

Don't settle for conterfeit love. Invite God to move in these areas.

MY WEEKLY GOALS

Jot down goals & activities for the week.

Love God

This week I will love God by:

☐

☐

☐

☐

☐

Love Neighbor

This week I will love my neighbors by:

☐

☐

☐

☐

☐

PRAISE & PRAYERS

Daily Prayers
Each morning and evening pray the daily prayers.

Praise
God, this week I praise you for:

☐

☐

☐

Personal Prayers
God, please move in these areas of my life this week:

☐

☐

☐

Prayers for Others
God, this week please move in the following neighbors lives:

☐

☐

☐

JOURNAL

SEND ME

Date: _____

VERSE OF THE WEEK

Then I heard the voice of the Lord saying, "Whom shall I send, and who will go for us?" And I said, "Here am I; send me!"

ISAIAH 6:8

READING PLAN

- ☐ 1 Thessalonians 5:23-28
- ☐ 2 Thessalonians 1
- ☐ 2 Thessalonians 2:1-3:5
- ☐ 2 Thessalonians 3:6-18
- ☐ 1 Timothy 1
- ☐ 1 Timothy 2
- ☐ Psalm 66
- ☐ Psalm 67
- ☐ Psalm 68

DEVOTIONAL THOUGHT

Read Isaiah 6:1-13

One of the most frustrating things for me is when someone says they care about or are committed to something but are unwilling to act on it. It can be maddening to watch as their behaviors prove a different set of values altogether. Words can be cheap. Flowing easily off the tongue, they are often mismatched with conviction and action on the part of the speaker.

When it comes to our relationship with God, the right things to say are "*I love you*" and "*Yes, I will follow you*". Given how obviously correct these things are, we can find ourselves saying these things quickly and easily. But do we match them with deeds?

If I told my wife I loved her but spent all my time with other women, do I really love her? If I told my kids I loved them but abandoned them, do I really love them? If I told my boss I was committed but never showed up at work, was I really committed?

Prove your love for the Lord by uniting your words with corresponding actions. Do justice. Love kindness. Walk humbly before Him.

REFLECT

Do your actions align with your professions of faith?

When the voice of the Lord is recruiting help, do you respond?

Where is God calling you to?

Reflect on what holds you back from going out on that mission.

MY WEEKLY GOALS

Jot down goals & activities for the week.

Love God
This week I will love God by:

☐

☐

☐

☐

☐

Love Neighbor
This week I will love my neighbors by:

☐

☐

☐

☐

☐

PRAISE & PRAYERS

Daily Prayers
Each morning and evening pray the daily prayers.

Praise
God, this week I praise you for:

☐

☐

☐

Personal Prayers
God, please move in these areas of my life this week:

☐

☐

☐

Prayers for Others
God, this week please move in the following neighbors lives:

☐

☐

☐

JOURNAL

CARRYING ONE ANOTHER

Date: _____

VERSE OF THE WEEK

Bear one another's burdens, and in this way you will fulfill the law of Christ.

GALATIANS 6:2

READING PLAN

☐ 1 Timothy 3
☐ 1 Timothy 4
☐ 1 Timothy 5:1-6:2

☐ 1 Timothy 6:3-21
☐ 2 Timothy 1:1-18
☐ Psalm 69

☐ Psalm 70
☐ Psalm 71

DEVOTIONAL THOUGHT

Read Galatians 6:1-10

Years ago, I was playing basketball and landed from a jump shot on the defender's foot. My ankle rolled and popped. While the shot went in, I damaged the tendon as it passes through the ankle and was on crutches for 6 months. I quickly discovered how critical community support is.

While caring for another can seem like a hassle at times, it is an embodiment of Kingdom principles. It moves us from an isolated existence into communal living. It moves us from self-reliance to mutual dependence. It moves us from greed to generosity.

Who in your life could use some help with their burdens this week? Could this be an opportunity not to serve but to make room for God to further transform your heart?

As you care for your neighbor, view this as an occasion to lean into the future of God's Kingdom. While His Kingdom is not fully realized, it has been inaugurated and can be experienced now.

REFLECT

Do you view yourself as a key, contributing member in the community that God has placed you in? Why or why not?

Contemplate a time when someone came to your aid and helped carry your burdens. How did that impact you?

What are some key ways you are positioned to support others?

Who in your life could use some support this week? Use this opportunity not simply to fulfill an obligation but to carry the burden's of a neighbor.

MY WEEKLY GOALS

Jot down goals & activities for the week.

Love God
This week I will love God by:

☐

☐

☐

☐

☐

Love Neighbor
This week I will love my neighbors by:

☐

☐

☐

☐

☐

PRAISE & PRAYERS

Daily Prayers

Each morning and evening pray the daily prayers.

Praise

God, this week I praise you for:

☐

☐

☐

Personal Prayers

God, please move in these areas of my life this week:

☐

☐

☐

Prayers for Others

God, this week please move in the following neighbors lives:

☐

☐

☐

JOURNAL

SHOW ME YOUR GLORY

Date: _____

VERSE OF THE WEEK

Moses said, "Show me your glory, I pray." And he said, "I will make all my goodness pass before you, and will proclaim before you the name, 'The Lord'; and I will be gracious to whom I will be gracious, and will show mercy on whom I will show mercy.

EXODUS 33:18-19

READING PLAN

- ☐ 2 Timothy 2
- ☐ 2 Timothy 3:1-9
- ☐ 2 Timothy 3:10-4:8
- ☐ 2 Timothy 4:9-22
- ☐ Titus 1
- ☐ Psalm 72
- ☐ Psalm 73
- ☐ Psalm 74

DEVOTIONAL THOUGHT

Read Exodus 33:12-23

Sometimes we know something is impressive, but we don't quite understand why or how. I know that a work of art, a book, or even a software program is impressive even if I cannot fully comprehend all that goes into it. I know that the universe is majestic even though I cannot see it all or wrap my head around it. Now and then, though, a piece of the puzzle falls into place to better appreciate a mystery.

On Mount Sinai, Moses asked God, "Show me your glory." God agreed to do so. Not only did it drive Moses to worship but it changed him. Having caught a glimpse of God's glory, Moses developed a greater appreciation for whom the Almighty was - even though he still could not fully comprehend Him.

Have you ever asked the Lord to reveal His glory to you? How might that change you? How might that draw you into worship? How might that increase your love for him?

Pray that God would reveal Himself to you this week. May you have a better understanding of who He is. May your knowledge move from your head to your heart. May you be more passionate. May spontaneous worship ignite inside of you. May your love for Him explode.

REFLECT

Think back to a time when your eyes were opened in a new way. How did that help you better appreciate the thing in question?

When did you last have a particularly intimate experience of God's glory? How did that encourage you in your faith? How did that help you love Jesus more deeply?

Would you like for the Lord to show you His glory? Seek that from Him.

Where are you seeing God move this week?

MY WEEKLY GOALS

Jot down goals & activities for the week.

Love God

This week I will love God by:

☐

☐

☐

☐

☐

Love Neighbor

This week I will love my neighbors by:

☐

☐

☐

☐

☐

PRAISE & PRAYERS

Daily Prayers
Each morning and evening pray the daily prayers.

Praise
God, this week I praise you for:

☐

☐

☐

Personal Prayers
God, please move in these areas of my life this week:

☐

☐

☐

Prayers for Others
God, this week please move in the following neighbors lives:

☐

☐

☐

JOURNAL

AS WE WOULD HAVE DONE TO US

Date: _____

VERSE OF THE WEEK

In everything do to others as you would have them do to you; for this is the law and the prophets.

MATTHEW 7:12

READING PLAN

- ☐ Titus 2
- ☐ Titus 3:1-11
- ☐ Titus 3:12-15
- ☐ Philemon 1
- ☐ Psalm 75
- ☐ Psalm 76
- ☐ Psalm 77

DEVOTIONAL THOUGHT

Read Matthew 7:12-29

Dealing with people can be challenging to say the least. Wouldn't it be easier if Jesus had said, "*Do unto others as they do unto you*"? Then we could merely show kindness to those that are treating us well -- currently. If someone mistreated us, we could turn around and do the same. In fact, this is how many people operate. Right?

However, Jesus calls us to proactively do good to one and all. Show kindness even in the face of hatred. Give to those in need regardless of context. Let the hurts done to you fade away. Seek the best even for your enemy.

Love your neighbor according to their circumstances, not yours.

May God grant you the strength and compassion to care for others as you would have them treat you.

REFLECT

Think back to a time when you wished someone else knew what you were going through. How frustrating was it that they could not understand your perspective?

Are you able to empathize well with others?

In moments of conflict, do you ever pause to think about what others are going through?

How might you re-train your responses in tense moments to ensure that you treat others as you would like to be treated?

MY WEEKLY GOALS

Jot down goals & activities for the week.

Love God

This week I will love God by:

☐

☐

☐

☐

☐

Love Neighbor

This week I will love my neighbors by:

☐

☐

☐

☐

☐

PRAISE & PRAYERS

Daily Prayers
Each morning and evening pray the daily prayers.

Praise
God, this week I praise you for:

☐

☐

☐

Personal Prayers
God, please move in these areas of my life this week:

☐

☐

☐

Prayers for Others
God, this week please move in the following neighbors lives:

☐

☐

☐

JOURNAL

CLOTHE YOURSELF

Date: _____

VERSE OF THE WEEK

As God's chosen ones, holy and beloved, clothe yourselves with compassion, kindness, humility, meekness, and patience.

COLOSSIANS 3:12

READING PLAN

☐ Matthew 1:1-17   ☐ Matthew 3   ☐ Psalm 79
☐ Matthew 1:18-2:12   ☐ Matthew 4:1-11   ☐ Psalm 80
☐ Matthew 2:13-23   ☐ Psalm 78

DEVOTIONAL THOUGHT

Read Colossians 3:1-17; Ephesians 4:17-32

It is always fun to watch kids dress up in their mom and dad's clothes when they are little. Watching them imitate and aspire to be like their parents is both cute and flattering. While they cannot quite fill out the clothes, it is fascinating to see how they appear like the parent. What a great way for the child to express their love for the parent!

We can express our love for our Almighty Father by clothing ourselves like Him. As we put on some of His key attributes - compassion, kindness, humility, gentleness, and patience - we respond to the love that He holds for us. We might not look exactly like Him. Yet, with time, we will start to look more and more like Him.

This week imitate your Heavenly Father's love by dressing yourself with the attributes that you see Him wearing. May you not just call Him Father. May you resemble Him to such a degree that people see Him in you.

REFLECT

Do you intentionally try to imitate God?

In what areas do you think you best reflect God? How? Celebrate the ways Jesus is already working in you!

What are some areas that you do not reflect God well in? Why is that?

How might you try to clothe yourself like Him in those areas you need to grow in?

MY WEEKLY GOALS

Jot down goals & activities for the week.

Love God

This week I will love God by:

☐

☐

☐

☐

☐

Love Neighbor

This week I will love my neighbors by:

☐

☐

☐

☐

☐

PRAISE & PRAYERS

Daily Prayers

Each morning and evening pray the daily prayers.

Praise

God, this week I praise you for:

☐

☐

☐

Personal Prayers

God, please move in these areas of my life this week:

☐

☐

☐

Prayers for Others

God, this week please move in the following neighbors lives:

☐

☐

☐

JOURNAL

HONOR OTHERS

Date: _____

VERSE OF THE WEEK

L et love be genuine; hate what is evil, hold fast to what is good; love one another with mutual affection; outdo one another in showing honor.

ROMANS 12:9-10

READING PLAN

☐ Matthew 4:12-25	☐ Matthew 6:1-18	☐ Psalm 81
☐ Matthew 5:1-16	☐ Matthew 6:19-24	☐ Psalm 82
☐ Matthew 5:17-48	☐ Matthew 6:25-34	☐ Psalm 83

DEVOTIONAL THOUGHT

Read Romans 12:9-21

He was livid. "*How could she have done that?*" he thought. "*What might have been going through her head?*" He wasn't just frustrated. He was angry. His opinion of her plummeted due to her supposed stupidity…. If only he had known what she was actually thinking. If only he had realized the factors he was unaware of. If only he had recognized the wisdom in her actions. If only he had respected and trusted her.

Our tendency is to criticize first and ask questions later. We often approach any circumstance where things do not go the way we expect or where things are done contrary to what we would have done ourselves as if the person at the other end of things is ignorant. We are often ill-informed and wrong. More importantly, we dishonor and debase that person.

As followers of Jesus we are called to value and honor others *above ourselves*. You see, others have the image of God in them. Others are cherished by God. If God loves and values these people, should we not follow suit?

Think of your latest frustrating encounter with someone. Can you imagine a scenario in which they might have had valid reasons for doing what they did? Now, ask yourself how God views this person? Does God care for that person? Does Jesus care for that person enough to humble and sacrifice Himself in order to redeem and restore that person? Consider how you might follow in His footsteps and adopt a similar view towards that person.

REFLECT

Do you generally give others the benefit of the doubt? Or are you quick to judge?

Consider if and how you extend the patience and grace that you wished others would give you.

Do you tend to view others through the lens of your personal experience with them or through the eyes of Jesus who loves them and wants to reconcile with them?

Do you consider yourself a prideful person? Do you tend to honor others above yourself (in and out of conflict)? Spend some time reflecting on what work you should allow God to do on your heart so that you can love your neighbors better.

MY WEEKLY GOALS

Jot down goals & activities for the week.

Love God

This week I will love God by:

☐

☐

☐

☐

☐

Love Neighbor

This week I will love my neighbors by:

☐

☐

☐

☐

☐

PRAISE & PRAYERS

Daily Prayers
Each morning and evening pray the daily prayers.

Praise
God, this week I praise you for:

☐

☐

☐

Personal Prayers
God, please move in these areas of my life this week:

☐

☐

☐

Prayers for Others
God, this week please move in the following neighbors lives:

☐

☐

☐

JOURNAL

DESIRING TO BE TOGETHER

Date: _____

VERSE OF THE WEEK

For to me, living is Christ and dying is gain. If I am to live in the flesh, that means fruitful labor for me; and I do not know which I prefer. I am hard pressed between the two: my desire is to depart and be with Christ, for that is far better; but to remain in the flesh is more necessary for you.

PHILIPPIANS 1:21-24

READING PLAN

☐ Matthew 7:1-12   ☐ Matthew 10   ☐ Psalm 85
☐ Matthew 7:13-29 ☐ Matthew 11   ☐ Psalm 86
☐ Matthew 8   ☐ Matthew 12
☐ Matthew 9   ☐ Psalm 84

DEVOTIONAL THOUGHT

Read Philippians 1:12-30

When my wife and I were first engaged, we found ourselves living 400 miles apart for several months. It was one of the hardest seasons of my life. Although there was a purpose to it, I longed to be near her.

The same ought to be true of our desire to be with the Lord. We should yearn to be with God. We should have a burning desire to experience His presence fully in heaven while also desiring to experience Him here and now. Thankfully, we can spend time with Emmanuel while on earth. However, to be united with Him in paradise will be much better than what we are able to encounter now.

Pray for an increased appetite for the presence of God. May you long to be fully present with Him.

May that desire fill you with hope. May that constantly draw you towards what lies ahead in eternity in a way that encourages you in your Kingdom work on earth.

REFLECT

Think back to a time when you desperately wanted to be back somewhere else (ie you were homesick or longing to be away on vacation). Was your mind somewhere else? How did that shape and focus your actions?

Do you long to be with Jesus? How so?

Are there places you desire to be more than in the presence of Jesus? Why do you think that is?

As Paul wrote this, he not only truly believed in Jesus but he knew how incredible paradise with Him would be. List out some thoughts as to why eternity with Jesus will be so incredible. Reflect on them each day this week.

MY WEEKLY GOALS

Jot down goals & activities for the week.

Love God
This week I will love God by:

☐

☐

☐

☐

☐

Love Neighbor
This week I will love my neighbors by:

☐

☐

☐

☐

☐

PRAISE & PRAYERS

Daily Prayers
Each morning and evening pray the daily prayers.

Praise
God, this week I praise you for:

☐

☐

☐

Personal Prayers
God, please move in these areas of my life this week:

☐

☐

☐

Prayers for Others
God, this week please move in the following neighbors lives:

☐

☐

☐

JOURNAL

LOVE IS PATIENT

Date: _____

VERSE OF THE WEEK

Love is patient; love is kind; love is not envious or boastful or arrogant or rude. It does not insist on its own way; it is not irritable or resentful; it does not rejoice in wrongdoing, but rejoices in the truth. It bears all things, believes all things, hopes all things, endures all things.

1 CORINTHIANS 13:4-7

READING PLAN

- ☐ Matthew 13
- ☐ Matthew 14
- ☐ Matthew 15
- ☐ Matthew 16
- ☐ Matthew 17
- ☐ Matthew 18
- ☐ Psalm 87
- ☐ Psalm 88
- ☐ Psalm 89

DEVOTIONAL THOUGHT

Read 1 Corinthians 13:1-13

"*Are we there yet?*" Parents and movie watchers alike are all too familiar with this phrase. Impatient children are unwilling to ride out the journey to the destination. They simply want to skip ahead to what awaits.

While children get a bad reputation for this saying, the reality is that the sentiment stays with most of us into adulthood. We might not use these exact words as we complain, but we certainly struggle with forbearance as we yearn for aspirations to be realized in our lives. This is especially true in our dealings with other people. We restlessly wait for others to mature and act the way we expect them to. Of course, we have little tolerance for those who will not give us that same space.

We are called to be patient with our neighbors. We are to bear with them as they work through issues, as they grow into spiritual maturity, and as they find their way. Surely we want those around us to look and act like Jesus. We are called, however, to extend them the grace they need on their journey, just as God is patient with us on our own meandering paths.

Extend more grace and bear with others this week. Pray that God would give you an extra measure of patience. Prepare yourself though. Prayers for patience often seem to produce opportunities to demonstrate patience.

REFLECT

Think back to some of the seasons of your life where you were particularly difficult to love. Who were some of the people in your life that were patient with you as you were figuring things out? Maybe thank them at some point this week for caring for you when you made it challenging.

Who in your life are you struggling to demonstrate patience towards? Who are you ready to give up on?

Why do you believe your patience is running thin? How might you find the strength to persevere in order to love those you are struggling with?

Imagine how powerful it might be if you calmly perservered and tolerated their wandering path to maturity. Pray for them and that your consistent, unwavering support would model the love of Jesus.

MY WEEKLY GOALS

Jot down goals & activities for the week.

Love God

This week I will love God by:

☐

☐

☐

☐

☐

Love Neighbor

This week I will love my neighbors by:

☐

☐

☐

☐

☐

PRAISE & PRAYERS

Daily Prayers
Each morning and evening pray the daily prayers.

Praise
God, this week I praise you for:

☐

☐

☐

Personal Prayers
God, please move in these areas of my life this week:

☐

☐

☐

Prayers for Others
God, this week please move in the following neighbors lives:

☐

☐

☐

JOURNAL

HOLD TIGHT TO HIS DEEDS

Date: _____

VERSE OF THE WEEK

When the Lord your God has brought you into the land that he swore to your ancestors, to Abraham, to Isaac, and to Jacob, to give you—a land with fine, large cities that you did not build, houses filled with all sorts of goods that you did not fill, hewn cisterns that you did not hew, vineyards and olive groves that you did not plant—and when you have eaten your fill, take care that you do not forget the Lord, who brought you out of the land of Egypt, out of the house of slavery.

DEUTERONOMY 6:10-12

READING PLAN

- ☐ Matthew 19:1-20:16
- ☐ Matthew 20:17-21:11
- ☐ Matthew 21:12-27
- ☐ Matthew 21:28-22:14
- ☐ Matthew 22:15-46
- ☐ Matthew 23
- ☐ Matthew 24
- ☐ Psalm 90
- ☐ Psalm 91
- ☐ Psalm 92

DEVOTIONAL THOUGHT

Read Deuteronomy 6:1-25

Have you ever forgotten why you were doing something? I feel like this happens every time I am in the middle of a run where I question why I am suffering through it. No longer remembering why I'm doing it, I find myself tempted to end the exercise early. In case you cannot tell, running is not my favorite workout. I have discovered that I need constant reminders in my life - even for those things that should be unforgettable.

We humans can have very short memories. That is compounded by questioning of things that occurs when adversity comes. For this reason, it is imperative that we hold on to those pivotal moments and key events, especially those great deeds that God has done.

I have seen God heal the sick. I've seen Him multiply food for those in need. I've seen Him perform miracles in my family. I've seen His perfect timing. I've seen His provision when it seemed that there was none to be had. Yet when adversity comes, I tend to forget. We must remind ourselves and hold tight to the remarkable deeds of the Almighty.

Jot down some of the ways God has positively affected your life and the lives of those around you. Review them each day this week and commit them to memory so that when the storms come you can stand fast and rest in the arms of the all-powerful, loving God.

REFLECT

In times of trial, do you tend to forget all that God has done for you in the past?

Why do you think your memory of God's faithfulness and goodness fades quickly? Spend some time this week ruminating on why that might be.

Jot down some of the ways God has moved in your life and the lives of those around you. Review them each day this week and commit them to memory so that when the storms come you can stand fast and rest in the arms of the all-powerful, loving God.

Where are you seeing God move this week?

MY WEEKLY GOALS

Jot down goals & activities for the week.

Love God
This week I will love God by:

☐

☐

☐

☐

☐

Love Neighbor
This week I will love my neighbors by:

☐

☐

☐

☐

☐

PRAISE & PRAYERS

Daily Prayers
Each morning and evening pray the daily prayers.

Praise
God, this week I praise you for:

☐

☐

☐

Personal Prayers
God, please move in these areas of my life this week:

☐

☐

☐

Prayers for Others
God, this week please move in the following neighbors lives:

☐

☐

☐

JOURNAL

LOVING IS FORGIVING

Date: _____

VERSE OF THE WEEK

Put away from you all bitterness and wrath and anger and wrangling and slander, together with all malice, and be kind to one another, tenderhearted, forgiving one another, as God in Christ has forgiven you.

EPHESIANS 4:31-32

READING PLAN

☐ Matthew 25	☐ Matthew 27:1-26	☐ Psalm 93
☐ Matthew 26:1-29	☐ Matthew 27:27-66	☐ Psalm 94
☐ Matthew 26:30-75	☐ Matthew 28	☐ Psalm 95

DEVOTIONAL THOUGHT

Read Ephesians 4:25-32

Reflect back on a time when you were deeply wounded by another. How did you feel? How did you respond? Now for the hard question: have you truly forgiven that person?

Forgiveness is one of the most challenging things for us humans to do. The deeper the wound the harder it is to forgive. In fact, the deeper the wound, the more justification we seem to have to be vindictive. Scripture is clear, however, that vengeance is not for us to partake in. Any repayment should be left to the Lord.

Moreover, if the holy, impeccable Lord is able to not just allow forgiveness but to actually seek it out, so should we. As flawed individuals ourselves who are the recipients of God's mercy, we are called to extend the same mercy and forgiveness to those that have wronged us - without exception.

Do not merely assent to forgive when forced to. Seek to grant it wherever needed from the heart.

REFLECT

How does discord sit with you? Do you actively seek reconcilation or do you avoid it? Why do you think that is?

Reflect on a time when you wronged someone else and they offering you forgiveness.

Who in your life have you not forgiven? Process why you have withheld forgiveness from these people.

If Jesus has forgiven those you have not forgiven, why haven't you? Make progress towards forgiveness today.

MY WEEKLY GOALS

Jot down goals & activities for the week.

Love God
This week I will love God by:

- [ ]

- [ ]

- [ ]

- [ ]

- [ ]

Love Neighbor
This week I will love my neighbors by:

- [ ]

- [ ]

- [ ]

- [ ]

- [ ]

PRAISE & PRAYERS

Daily Prayers

Each morning and evening pray the daily prayers.

Praise

God, this week I praise you for:

☐

☐

☐

Personal Prayers

God, please move in these areas of my life this week:

☐

☐

☐

Prayers for Others

God, this week please move in the following neighbors lives:

☐

☐

☐

JOURNAL

SERVING THE ONE WE LOVE

Date: _____

VERSE OF THE WEEK

So now, O Israel, what does the Lord your God require of you? Only to fear the Lord your God, to walk in all his ways, to love him, to serve the Lord your God with all your heart and with all your soul, and to keep the commandments of the Lord your God and his decrees that I am commanding you today, for your own well-being.

DEUTERONOMY 10:12-13

READING PLAN

☐ Hebrews 1
☐ Hebrews 2
☐ Hebrews 3:1-6
☐ Hebrews 3:7-4:13
☐ Hebrews 4:14-5:10
☐ Hebrews 5:11-6:20
☐ Hebrews 7
☐ Psalm 96
☐ Psalm 97
☐ Psalm 98

DEVOTIONAL THOUGHT

Read Deuteronomy 10:12-22

The more we love someone, the more our hearts desire to see them, experience wholeness, and accomplish their goals. As we become aligned with and passionate about them, we find ourselves committed to their success. This internal connection results in external action.

As we fall in love with the Lord to whom belong the heavens and the earth, who saved us, who cares for us, and who reigns over all things, we should start to experience a love for Him that precipitates movement. We should find ourselves serving Him and doing what we can to advance His purposes.

It's not that God needs us to build His Kingdom. Rather, He chooses to invite us into His purposes. Our adoration for and commitment to Him should propel us to join with Him and build for His

Kingdom.

In what ways do you serve the Lord? Do you desire to serve Him or do you merely do it out of a sense of duty? How might you serve the God you love with your time and talents in the coming weeks?

REFLECT

In what ways do you currently serve the Lord? Reflect on your motivations for doing it.

How does it make you feel when you serve Him?

In what ways is God calling you to serve Him that you are not currently following through on?

Are you willing to step out in faith out of a love for Jesus?

MY WEEKLY GOALS

Jot down goals & activities for the week.

Love God

This week I will love God by:

☐

☐

☐

☐

☐

Love Neighbor

This week I will love my neighbors by:

☐

☐

☐

☐

☐

PRAISE & PRAYERS

Daily Prayers

Each morning and evening pray the daily prayers.

Praise

God, this week I praise you for:

☐

☐

☐

Personal Prayers

God, please move in these areas of my life this week:

☐

☐

☐

Prayers for Others

God, this week please move in the following neighbors lives:

☐

☐

☐

JOURNAL

BUILD OTHERS UP

Date: _____

VERSE OF THE WEEK

Therefore encourage one another and build up each other, as indeed you are doing.

1 THESSALONIANS 5:11

READING PLAN

- [ ] Hebrews 8:1-9:10
- [ ] Hebrews 9:11-10:18
- [ ] Hebrews 10:19-39
- [ ] Hebrews 11:1-12:2
- [ ] Hebrews 12:3-29
- [ ] Hebrews 13:1-25
- [ ] Psalm 99
- [ ] Psalm 100
- [ ] Psalm 101

DEVOTIONAL THOUGHT

Read 1 Thessalonians 5:1-11

I remember that I had a phase in middle school where I thought it was cool to tear people down. A witty "burn" was sure to bring a laugh. It would elevate my status in the group as I put others down - at least that is what it felt like. Of course, it didn't feel so good when I was on the other end of that.

It was only later in life that I truly discovered the call to build others up. To be human in the manner that God created us is to use our blessings and opportunities to edify others. We are blessed to be a blessing. Uplifting words and deeds hold immense power to change the world and show God's love to others.

Do you seek to build others up? Where might an intentional effort edify others fit in your life? Reflect on the various circles of your life and consider how God might use you to encourage others in their faith journey.

REFLECT

Do your words generally build others up or tear them down?

Compare the impact of some recent edifying vs negative words you have spoken to others. Consider the power your tongue wields.

Who is someone that has brought key encouragement to you? How impactful have their words been in your life?

Who in your life could use some encouragement this week? Pray that God would reveal some discouraged neighbors to you. Reach out to them and speak life into them.

MY WEEKLY GOALS

Jot down goals & activities for the week.

Love God
This week I will love God by:

☐

☐

☐

☐

☐

Love Neighbor
This week I will love my neighbors by:

☐

☐

☐

☐

☐

PRAISE & PRAYERS

Daily Prayers
Each morning and evening pray the daily prayers.

Praise
God, this week I praise you for:

☐

☐

☐

Personal Prayers
God, please move in these areas of my life this week:

☐

☐

☐

Prayers for Others
God, this week please move in the following neighbors lives:

☐

☐

☐

JOURNAL

ABIDE IN LOVE

Date: _____

VERSE OF THE WEEK

By this we know that we abide in him and he in us, because he has given us of his Spirit. And we have seen and do testify that the Father has sent his Son as the Savior of the world. God abides in those who confess that Jesus is the Son of God, and they abide in God. So we have known and believe the love that God has for us.

1 John 4:13-16

READING PLAN

- ☐ Mark 1
- ☐ Mark 2-3
- ☐ Mark 4:1-34
- ☐ Mark 4:35-5:43
- ☐ Mark 6
- ☐ Psalm 102
- ☐ Psalm 103
- ☐ Psalm 104

DEVOTIONAL THOUGHT

Read 1 John 4:7-21

The plants kept withering and dying. I could not figure out why. Time and again it would happen. I would delicately plant a nice seedling, surround it with soil amendment, and hope for the best. But it would struggle. It lacked the strength to survive, let alone thrive. Only later did I discover that the plants were unable to pull up the proper water and nutrients from the ground as it was planted in hard, clay-filled soil. I may not have been supplying the proper amount of water as well. As a result, they did not have a proper source from which to grow.

Do you ever feel like you lack the spiritual nutrients and energy to thrive in your faith? Perhaps you feel like you are barely surviving or are decaying even.

I have good news for you. You do not have to find the strength to be a spiritual superhero from your inner self. You do not have to manufacture a loving heart entirely on your own. Instead, you can allow the love of God to flow through you. Like a plant drawing nutrients from rich soil, you can extract spiritual strength, joy, and love from the ultimate source of love. God is love. If you abide in Him, you can rely on His love.

Turn to the source of love. Abide in Him. Allow the love of Jesus to flow through your veins and to flow out of your lungs.

REFLECT

Do you often find yourself drained? Do you lack for the spiritual energy to press forward into this calling to love?

Where do you feel the most exhausted?

How have you cut yourself of from the source of life and love? What practices have you removed that once provided a conduit to the love of Jesus?

What might you do to connect or reconnect with the love of Jesus? The point is not to find the strength to do more. The point is to connect with Jesus so that He might do more through you.

MY WEEKLY GOALS

Jot down goals & activities for the week.

Love God

This week I will love God by:

☐

☐

☐

☐

☐

Love Neighbor

This week I will love my neighbors by:

☐

☐

☐

☐

☐

PRAISE & PRAYERS

Daily Prayers
Each morning and evening pray the daily prayers.

Praise
God, this week I praise you for:

☐

☐

☐

Personal Prayers
God, please move in these areas of my life this week:

☐

☐

☐

Prayers for Others
God, this week please move in the following neighbors lives:

☐

☐

☐

JOURNAL

PERFECTED IN US

Date: _____

VERSE OF THE WEEK

No one has ever seen God; if we love one another, God lives in us, and his love is perfected in us.

1 JOHN 4:12

READING PLAN

- [ ] Mark 7:1-8:26
- [ ] Mark 8:27-9:50
- [ ] Mark 10
- [ ] Mark 11
- [ ] Mark 12
- [ ] Mark 13
- [ ] Mark 14
- [ ] Psalm 105
- [ ] Psalm 106
- [ ] Psalm 107

DEVOTIONAL THOUGHT

Read 1 John 4:7-12

"It is no longer I who live but Christ who lives in me." One of the great mysteries of the faith is how exactly God dwells inside of us. While we are not likely to fully understand the inner workings of this, we do know that when God dwells in us, we find ourselves reflecting Him and loving others more. As we love our neighbors, not only is it an expression of what is inside of us, but it allows God's love to be perfected in us.

The Greek word for perfect implies completeness. As we love others, His love is further completed in us. With each sincere act of love, we allow the image of God inside of us to be seen to a greater degree and we allow Him to further transform us into His loving reflection.

As someone in whom Jesus dwells, allow Him to take over. Allow Him to shine through. Allow His love to be expressed in and through you. Allow His love to be perfected in you.

REFLECT

Would others say that the love of God is evident in you?

How does it make you feel to think that God's love might be perfected in you? Do you even feel that is possible?

If God's love is perfected in you as you love others, who might you demonstrate love to this week that the love of God might flow through you? How might you demonstrate that love to them? Be specific.

Where are you seeing God move this week?

MY WEEKLY GOALS

Jot down goals & activities for the week.

Love God

This week I will love God by:

☐

☐

☐

☐

☐

Love Neighbor

This week I will love my neighbors by:

☐

☐

☐

☐

☐

PRAISE & PRAYERS

Daily Prayers
Each morning and evening pray the daily prayers.

Praise
God, this week I praise you for:

☐

☐

☐

Personal Prayers
God, please move in these areas of my life this week:

☐

☐

☐

Prayers for Others
God, this week please move in the following neighbors lives:

☐

☐

☐

JOURNAL

HIM ALONE

Date: _____

VERSE OF THE WEEK

The Lord your God you shall follow, him alone you shall fear, his commandments you shall keep, his voice you shall obey, him you shall serve, and to him you shall hold fast.

DEUTERONOMY 13:4

READING PLAN

- ☐ Mark 15
- ☐ Mark 16
- ☐ 1 Peter 1:1-12
- ☐ 1 Peter 1:13-2:3
- ☐ 1 Peter 2:4-10
- ☐ 1 Peter 2:11-3:12
- ☐ Psalm 108
- ☐ Psalm 109
- ☐ Psalm 110

DEVOTIONAL THOUGHT

Read Deuteronomy 13:1-9

The concept of following other gods seems very strange to me. To abandon Jesus in order to follow a god named Baal whom I would worship as a piece of bull-shaped metal, for example, does not quite make sense for me.

However, as we dig deeper, we discover that the gods that seduced the people away from God represented fertility, harvest, or other things that promised to improve their lives. We see that they promised to fulfill the desires of their hearts.

While you may not be enticed by gods with other names or that can rest lifelessly on a shelf, are you tempted by the gods of self-reliance, sex, prosperity, pleasure, knowledge, or greed? These things, however well packaged they may appear, not only have empty promises of wholeness but would pull you away from the God that has your best interests at heart.

Will you love God to the point that you will entrust Him with your life? Will you love Him to the point that you will not seek alternative solutions that pull you away from His plans for you?

May you have the discernment to identify the would-be gods that might impair your commitment to the Almighty. May you love Jesus and Jesus alone.

REFLECT

What or who do you put your trust in? Why do these things make you feel secure?

Do you feel that these alternatives offer true security? Where do they fall short?

What causes you to take your eyes and heart off of the Lord?

How might you put your trust in God alone, reprioritizing all else after Him?

MY WEEKLY GOALS

Jot down goals & activities for the week.

Love God

This week I will love God by:

☐

☐

☐

☐

☐

Love Neighbor

This week I will love my neighbors by:

☐

☐

☐

☐

☐

PRAISE & PRAYERS

Daily Prayers
Each morning and evening pray the daily prayers.

Praise
God, this week I praise you for:

☐

☐

☐

Personal Prayers
God, please move in these areas of my life this week:

☐

☐

☐

Prayers for Others
God, this week please move in the following neighbors lives:

☐

☐

☐

JOURNAL

LOVE SHARES

Date: _____

VERSE OF THE WEEK

And the crowds asked him, "What then should we do?" In reply he said to them, "Whoever has two coats must share with anyone who has none; and whoever has food must do likewise."

LUKE 3:10-11

READING PLAN

- ☐ 1 Peter 3:13-4:19
- ☐ 1 Peter 5
- ☐ 2 Peter 1
- ☐ 2 Peter 2
- ☐ 2 Peter 3
- ☐ Romans 1:1-17
- ☐ Psalm 111
- ☐ Psalm 112
- ☐ Psalm 113

DEVOTIONAL THOUGHT

Read Luke 3:10-14

When we have $1 to our name, we seek $2. When we have $10, we seek $20. When we have $1,000, we seek $2,000. And so on. Never content, we continually accumulate what we can. While there is biblical wisdom in building up savings, we are not called to view ourselves in a solitary battle against the world. We are called to see ourselves as part of humanity. We are to be a contributing component of God's creation.

When we view assets and wealth from an eternal or the spiritual perspective, we realize that they are tools to advance God's kingdom. The beauty of it is that when all are operating in this way, we might provide for the one who lacks out of our own abundance today, whereas someone else's abundance might provide for our needs tomorrow. Additionally, we realize that in the Kingdom of God, there is always abundance.

What assets has God given you that you can share with those in need? What fears prevent you from walking more generously? Where do you see needs around you that you can meet?

REFLECT

Do you tend to operate in a mindset of scarcity or abundance?

How does your mindset impact how you share with other?

Do you typically view the resources you have as tools for God's Kingdom or assets for your own stockpiling and consumption? Why?

Think of someone in need. Do you have the means to help them? Do you trust the Lord enough to do so?

MY WEEKLY GOALS

Jot down goals & activities for the week.

Love God

This week I will love God by:

☐

☐

☐

☐

☐

Love Neighbor

This week I will love my neighbors by:

☐

☐

☐

☐

☐

PRAISE & PRAYERS

Daily Prayers
Each morning and evening pray the daily prayers.

Praise
God, this week I praise you for:

☐

☐

☐

Personal Prayers
God, please move in these areas of my life this week:

☐

☐

☐

Prayers for Others
God, this week please move in the following neighbors lives:

☐

☐

☐

JOURNAL

CONTINUAL PURSUIT

Date: _____

VERSE OF THE WEEK

Seek the Lord and his strength,
seek his presence continually.

1 CHRONICLES 16:11

READING PLAN

☐ Romans 1:18-32   ☐ Romans 3:9-20   ☐ Psalm 114
☐ Romans 2:1-16   ☐ Romans 3:21-31   ☐ Psalm 115
☐ Romans 2:17-3:8   ☐ Romans 4   ☐ Psalm 116

DEVOTIONAL THOUGHT

Read 1 Chronicles 16:7-36

Sometimes I feel like my most common task as a father is to find the things that my children lose. I am frequently asked to help find something. As I question if they themselves have searched, it is clear that only a cursory effort was made. To be fair, I was the same way. My mother would say that I would have to pay her a quarter if she found the item first. I would immediately redouble my efforts.

Many feel that the moment we start to search for God He will appear. Whether or not that happens, most of us stop - either satisfied with a single encounter or disappointed that our brief effort failed. If we truly love the Lord, however, we will seek him continually. This is a concerted, ongoing effort to experience more and more of that which we desire - ***namely God***.

Do you give up your search for God easily? Do you settle for short encounters? This week, seek the Lord in the morning, afternoon, and night. Chase after His presence through the day, each and every day. See how He responds. As you experience Him, do not relent. Desire more. Continue your pursuit.

REFLECT

Do you tend to give up quickly or persevere until you attain your goals?

What things are you most persistent with? Why do you think that is?

Do you diligently pursue God's presence? Why do you think that is?

What impact might stem from continual seeking the Lord?

MY WEEKLY GOALS

Jot down goals & activities for the week.

Love God

This week I will love God by:

☐

☐

☐

☐

☐

Love Neighbor

This week I will love my neighbors by:

☐

☐

☐

☐

☐

PRAISE & PRAYERS

Daily Prayers
Each morning and evening pray the daily prayers.

Praise
God, this week I praise you for:

☐

☐

☐

Personal Prayers
God, please move in these areas of my life this week:

☐

☐

☐

Prayers for Others
God, this week please move in the following neighbors lives:

☐

☐

☐

JOURNAL

IT'S ABOUT THE HEART

Date: _____

VERSE OF THE WEEK

And if I have prophetic powers, and understand all mysteries and all knowledge, and if I have all faith, so as to remove mountains, but do not have love, I am nothing. If I give away all my possessions, and if I hand over my body so that I may boast, but do not have love, I gain nothing.

1 CORINTHIANS 13:2-3

READING PLAN

- ☐ Romans 5:1-11
- ☐ Romans 5:12-21
- ☐ Romans 6
- ☐ Romans 7
- ☐ Romans 8:1-17
- ☐ Romans 8:18-39
- ☐ Romans 9:1-29
- ☐ Psalm 117
- ☐ Psalm 118

DEVOTIONAL THOUGHT

Read 1 Corinthians 13

There is this phrase that we sometimes like to use in the church: "*to love on someone*". There is a powerful aspect to it that captures the idea that love without action is dead. Love is a verb. Love is something that is lived out.

However, it could be confused with the idea that love is only about action and not about sentiment. To lose the caring aspect of love is to lose love itself. To perform acts of justice, mercy, and kindness without actually having love misses the point. Moreover, they are empty. There is no value to them.

When you do good to your neighbors as an outflow of love, it is powerful. May your heart be filled with love for others. May that love be the catalyst for your actions.

Let love be at the center of all that you do. Where you lack love, pray that God would mold your heart and fill it with a passion for and commitment to those around you.

REFLECT

How often do you do things that feel hollow? Why do you do them?

Do you feel that your love for others is empty at times? Where do you most feel like this?

Where does your love feel most authentic? Where does it best flow from your heart?

How might you allow love to be the source of your actions? Pray that God work in your heart that it might be a spring of love from which authentic, Kingdom actions flow.

MY WEEKLY GOALS
Jot down goals & activities for the week.

Love God
This week I will love God by:

☐

☐

☐

☐

☐

Love Neighbor
This week I will love my neighbors by:

☐

☐

☐

☐

☐

PRAISE & PRAYERS

Daily Prayers

Each morning and evening pray the daily prayers.

Praise

God, this week I praise you for:

☐

☐

☐

Personal Prayers

God, please move in these areas of my life this week:

☐

☐

☐

Prayers for Others

God, this week please move in the following neighbors lives:

☐

☐

☐

JOURNAL

AN INTIMATE RELATIONSHIP

Date: _____

VERSE OF THE WEEK

I do not call you servants any longer, because the servant does not know what the master is doing; but I have called you friends, because I have made known to you everything that I have heard from my Father.

JOHN 15:15

READING PLAN

- ☐ Romans 9:30-10:21
- ☐ Romans 11
- ☐ Romans 12
- ☐ Romans 13
- ☐ Romans 14
- ☐ Romans 15:1-13
- ☐ Psalm 119:1-64
- ☐ Psalm 119:65-128
- ☐ Psalm 119:129-176

DEVOTIONAL THOUGHT

Read John 15:1-17

In theology, we speak of the transcendence and the immanence of God. The transcendence of God, in short, means that He is over and above all things. It emphasizes that God is separate from creation and not dependent upon it. The immanence of God focuses on His presence within creation, especially to humans. We see this in His name Emmanuel - God is with us.

Due to the grandeur and power of God, many of us focus on His transcendence. While this is an important trait, we often forget about His immanence. Yet, we see that God is not only present and available to His people, but He desires to walk in an intimate relationship with them. He does not desire to be a distant God that is known only as master and judge. He desires an affectionate relationship with His children. He not only desires to be your Lord and Savior, but your friend as well.

Do you view God as your friend? Do you walk in a warm and loving relationship with Jesus? Love for

God is not merely found in our gratitude, obedience, or response to God. Love for God can be friendly, personal, and intimate. Invite God into the innermost parts of your heart and develop a warm, caring relationship with Him.

REFLECT

Reflect on the difference between your closest, most intimate relationships and mere acquaintances where you have more of a transactional relationship.

How does it make you feel to think that the Most High God wants to have an intimate, personal, friendly relationship with you?

Do you want an intimate, personal, friendly relationship with Jesus?

What is one step that you could take to draw closer to Him?

MY WEEKLY GOALS

Jot down goals & activities for the week.

Love God

This week I will love God by:

☐

☐

☐

☐

☐

Love Neighbor

This week I will love my neighbors by:

☐

☐

☐

☐

☐

PRAISE & PRAYERS

Daily Prayers

Each morning and evening pray the daily prayers.

Praise

God, this week I praise you for:

☐

☐

☐

Personal Prayers

God, please move in these areas of my life this week:

☐

☐

☐

Prayers for Others

God, this week please move in the following neighbors lives:

☐

☐

☐

JOURNAL

AS GOD HAS LOVED US

Date: _____

VERSE OF THE WEEK

I give you a new commandment, that you love one another. Just as I have loved you, you also should love one another.

JOHN 13:34

READING PLAN

- ☐ Romans 15:14-33
- ☐ Romans 16
- ☐ James 1
- ☐ James 2
- ☐ James 3
- ☐ Psalm 120
- ☐ Psalm 121

DEVOTIONAL THOUGHT

Read John 13:31-35

Did you ever have one of those classes in school that you just did the bare minimum to get the desired grade - and not an ounce of effort more? I generally liked and did well in school. However, a few of the classes were not the least bit interesting for me and I had zero desire to do anything more than the minimum to get by.

We can be tempted to live the same way with our faith, especially when it comes to showing love to others. The expectation is not that we do the bare minimum though. Rather, we are called to love others just as Jesus showed love towards us. This was not a do-what-is-needed-to-get-by kind of love. This was an all-out, above and beyond, hold-nothing-back kind of love. This was a sacrificial love. This type of love continually asks, "*Is there anything more I can do?*" instead of "*what else must I do?*" There is a massive difference between the two.

This week hold nothing back from your love for others. Ask yourself what more you can do to care for and extend God's love to those you encounter.

REFLECT

Reflect for a moment. Do you tend to aim for the bare minimum in faith? Do you overflow with love
for God and others or do you hold back?

Do you dwell on the love of God for you? How often do you celebrate all He has done for you?

Does the love of God spur you on to greater love for others?

Contemplate the immense love Jesus has for you. Now, consider how you can appropriately respond
to that love.

MY WEEKLY GOALS

Jot down goals & activities for the week.

Love God

This week I will love God by:

☐

☐

☐

☐

☐

Love Neighbor

This week I will love my neighbors by:

☐

☐

☐

☐

☐

PRAISE & PRAYERS

Daily Prayers
Each morning and evening pray the daily prayers.

Praise
God, this week I praise you for:

☐

☐

☐

Personal Prayers
God, please move in these areas of my life this week:

☐

☐

☐

Prayers for Others
God, this week please move in the following neighbors lives:

☐

☐

☐

JOURNAL

TRANSFORMED IN HIS IMAGE

Date: _____

VERSE OF THE WEEK

Do not be conformed to this world, but be transformed by the renewing of your minds, so that you may discern what is the will of God—what is good and acceptable and perfect.

ROMANS 12:2

READING PLAN

- ☐ James 4:1-5:12
- ☐ James 5:13-20
- ☐ John 1
- ☐ John 2
- ☐ Psalm 122
- ☐ Psalm 123
- ☐ Psalm 124

DEVOTIONAL THOUGHT

Read Romans 12:1-8

When my wife and I first met in college, we were very different. Obviously, there was enough commonality there to form a bond. However, we had different backgrounds, different majors, and different interests. Fast forward twenty years and we have so much more in common. As time is spent together and our bond grows, we are more and more aligned. We even owned the same style of glasses!

A similar principle is true of our relationship with God. The more we love Him, the more time we spend with Him, the more we start to look like Him. Now, a key difference is that we were actually created in His image. The more we spend time with Him, the more that image is reclaimed in us.

Allow yourself to be transformed into the image of the God who so loved the world that He gave His only son. This will open your eyes to see the ways of His Kingdom and participate in it. What better way is there to love God than to walk in His ways, take part in His Kingdom, and reflect His love to the world?

REFLECT

Do you look like the God in whose image you were created? Or do you look more like the world around you?

Do you reflect Jesus better today than you did a year ago? In what ways?

What are some key areas that you need to be further transformed into the image of God?

What, if anything, are you going to do to pursue being transformed in the image of God? What practices will you put in place to create conditions for transformation and growth?

MY WEEKLY GOALS

Jot down goals & activities for the week.

Love God

This week I will love God by:

☐

☐

☐

☐

☐

Love Neighbor

This week I will love my neighbors by:

☐

☐

☐

☐

☐

PRAISE & PRAYERS

Daily Prayers
Each morning and evening pray the daily prayers.

Praise
God, this week I praise you for:

☐

☐

☐

Personal Prayers
God, please move in these areas of my life this week:

☐

☐

☐

Prayers for Others
God, this week please move in the following neighbors lives:

☐

☐

☐

JOURNAL

TO THOSE THAT HATE US

Date: _____

VERSE OF THE WEEK

But I say to you that listen, Love your enemies, do good to those who hate you, bless those who curse you, pray for those who abuse you.

LUKE 6:27-28

READING PLAN

- ☐ John 3:1-21
- ☐ John 3:22-36
- ☐ John 4:1-42
- ☐ John 4:43-5:18
- ☐ John 5:19-47
- ☐ John 6:1-21
- ☐ Psalm 125
- ☐ Psalm 126
- ☐ Psalm 127

DEVOTIONAL THOUGHT

Read Luke 6:27-31

By and large, I am a rule follower. I do not like to break the law or go against established rules. I expect the same of others in turn. My sense of justice, then, would have all rule breakers receive the full punishment they deserve.

Thank God that He didn't do to me as I would have done to others!

When it comes to ourselves, many of us want the mercy of God but not the justice of God. However, when it comes to others we often feel the opposite. We often want others to experience the consequences of justice and be excluded from mercy - especially when their infractions harmed us in some way.

When the love of God infiltrates our hearts, mercy and forgiveness take over and vengefulness starts to fade. Sometimes, we like to hang on to that spite though. Who are your enemies? Who are you unable to love because of what they have done to you?

Reflect on how God treated you when you were still His enemy. Pray that God would transform your heart to extend grace, mercy, and forgiveness to your enemies. Pray that He would help you love your enemies as He loves them.

REFLECT

Are you quick to forgive? Or is it a struggle to extend forgiveness to others? Why?

How does it make you feel that Jesus offered you forgiveness even when you did not deserve it?

Are you willing to show love and offer love even to your worst enemy?

What is a one step you can take towards loving those that hate you this week? How will that make a difference?

MY WEEKLY GOALS

Jot down goals & activities for the week.

Love God

This week I will love God by:

☐

☐

☐

☐

☐

Love Neighbor

This week I will love my neighbors by:

☐

☐

☐

☐

☐

PRAISE & PRAYERS

Daily Prayers

Each morning and evening pray the daily prayers.

Praise

God, this week I praise you for:

☐

☐

☐

Personal Prayers

God, please move in these areas of my life this week:

☐

☐

☐

Prayers for Others

God, this week please move in the following neighbors lives:

☐

☐

☐

JOURNAL

IN HIS WINGS

Date: _____

VERSE OF THE WEEK

For he will deliver you from the snare of the fowler and from the deadly pestilence; he will cover you with his pinions, and under his wings you will find refuge; his faithfulness is a shield and buckler.

PSALM 91:3-4

READING PLAN

- ☐ John 6:22-71
- ☐ John 7
- ☐ John 8
- ☐ John 9
- ☐ John 10:1-18
- ☐ John 10:19-42
- ☐ Psalm 128
- ☐ Psalm 129
- ☐ Psalm 130

DEVOTIONAL THOUGHT

Read Psalm 91

Feeling overworked and overwhelmed? The storms of life are not only relentless at times but can leave us vulnerable and defenseless. Our own strength, ingenuity, and resources are not enough to keep us safe.

One of the tenderest metaphors we see in Scripture is that of God as the mother bird that wraps its wings around its young ones. Just as the bird offers shelter and protection to her young, God offers you security and rest in His arms.

In the midst of the busyness, chaos, and storms of life, rest in the wings of the caring God who offers you safe haven. Sometimes we need to stop racing, stop fixing, stop working, and simply rest in the embrace of the Lord.

Allow God to cradle you in His powerful yet delicate wings. Feel the depth of His love for you. Relax in His care and protection.

REFLECT

Do you feel weary? Stressed? Attacked? Overwhelmed? Where do you feel that the most?

Do you feel like you deal with those emotions alone?

Do you know that God is your protector? Do you believe it? Do you feel it?

Will you allow yourself to rest in the arms of Jesus?

MY WEEKLY GOALS

Jot down goals & activities for the week.

Love God

This week I will love God by:

☐

☐

☐

☐

☐

Love Neighbor

This week I will love my neighbors by:

☐

☐

☐

☐

☐

PRAISE & PRAYERS

Daily Prayers
Each morning and evening pray the daily prayers.

Praise
God, this week I praise you for:

☐

☐

☐

Personal Prayers
God, please move in these areas of my life this week:

☐

☐

☐

Prayers for Others
God, this week please move in the following neighbors lives:

☐

☐

☐

JOURNAL

BEARING WITH

Date: _____

VERSE OF THE WEEK

Bear with one another and, if anyone has a complaint against another, forgive each other; just as the Lord has forgiven you, so you also must forgive.

COLOSSIANS 3:13

READING PLAN

- ☐ John 11:1-54
- ☐ John 11:55-12:19
- ☐ John 12:20-50
- ☐ John 13
- ☐ John 14
- ☐ John 15:1-17
- ☐ Psalm 131
- ☐ Psalm 132
- ☐ Psalm 133

DEVOTIONAL THOUGHT

Read Colossians 3:1-17

Too many times, I have watched as a small grievance destroys a relationship. Unable to extend forgiveness, the relationship is crushed under the weight of the offense that was committed. Like a balloon that continues to be inflated without relief, the pressure of an inability to forgive and bear with one another increases until things burst.

This makes sense for those who have not experienced the forgiveness of the Father. However, as recipients of Jesus' forgiveness, we are called to forgive others. To be clear, we are not called to forgive only if the wrong belonged to a certain category or if the repentance and retribution met certain criteria. There are no qualifications. As a people that could not receive greater mercy, we are to offer that same limitless mercy to others.

Are you annoyed at someone? Bear with them. Do you have a complaint about something that was done to you? Forgive that person. Extend forgiveness to relieve the pressure and allow the forgiveness of Jesus to dwell in your heart without exception or qualification.

REFLECT

How have you felt as you witnessed others' relationships torn apart?

When you are frustrated, angry or livid with others, do you bear with them? Or do you cast them aside?

How might you view these situations though the eyes of Jesus?

Who do you need to bear with this week? Pray that God would allow you to love them even when that is difficult.

MY WEEKLY GOALS

Jot down goals & activities for the week.

Love God

This week I will love God by:

☐

☐

☐

☐

☐

Love Neighbor

This week I will love my neighbors by:

☐

☐

☐

☐

☐

PRAISE & PRAYERS

Daily Prayers

Each morning and evening pray the daily prayers.

Praise

God, this week I praise you for:

☐

☐

☐

Personal Prayers

God, please move in these areas of my life this week:

☐

☐

☐

Prayers for Others

God, this week please move in the following neighbors lives:

☐

☐

☐

JOURNAL

WALKING ON HIS PATH

Date: _____

VERSE OF THE WEEK

Trust in the Lord with all your heart, and do not rely on your own insight. In all your ways acknowledge him, and he will make straight your paths.

PROVERBS 3:5-6

READING PLAN

- ☐ John 15:18-16:15
- ☐ John 16:16-33
- ☐ John 17
- ☐ John 18:1-27
- ☐ John 18:28-19:16
- ☐ John 19:17-42
- ☐ Psalm 134
- ☐ Psalm 135
- ☐ Psalm 136

DEVOTIONAL THOUGHT

Read Proverbs 3:1-12

We were making incredible time. I don't recall too many times when I have hiked at a faster pace. We were moving so much faster than anyone else in the group. I was so proud of myself. We were going to arrive at the camp before everyone else. Well, that's what I had thought at least. We had disregarded the map and signs and walked miles in the wrong direction before realizing it. As I recall, we walked into camp last - weary and soaked from the storm that had rolled in during the delay.

Walking on the right path is key - whether speaking literally or metaphorically. Too often we miss or deliberately ignore the signposts that send us in the right direction. We can love the Lord by trusting His ways over ours and walking down the paths He leads us down.

Ask yourself where you have been resisting the places that God has been calling you to. Whether pride, selfishness, self-reliance or something else, what is the source of the resistance? How can you love God this week by entrusting your life's steps to Him?

REFLECT

Have you ever gone down the wrong path (literally or figuratively)? How frustrating was it? How did it impact you?

How have you been walking in the ways of Jesus? Take some time this week to celebrate the progress you have made and the blessings that have resulted from this.

Where do you struggle to walk on the right path? Why do you think that is?

Do you trust God enough that you are willing to walk down His path? Do you trust Him enough that you will follow His ways even when you do not understand them or know where they are leading? Ruminate on this honestly.

MY WEEKLY GOALS

Jot down goals & activities for the week.

Love God

This week I will love God by:

☐

☐

☐

☐

☐

Love Neighbor

This week I will love my neighbors by:

☐

☐

☐

☐

☐

PRAISE & PRAYERS

Daily Prayers
Each morning and evening pray the daily prayers.

Praise
God, this week I praise you for:

☐

☐

☐

Personal Prayers
God, please move in these areas of my life this week:

☐

☐

☐

Prayers for Others
God, this week please move in the following neighbors lives:

☐

☐

☐

JOURNAL

LOVE AS SACRIFICE

Date: _____

VERSE OF THE WEEK

No one has greater love than this, to lay down one's life for one's friends.

John 15:13

READING PLAN

☐ John 20
☐ John 21
☐ 1 John 1:1-2:6
☐ 1 John 2:7-17

☐ 1 John 2:18-3:3
☐ 1 John 3:4-24
☐ 1 John 4
☐ Psalm 137

☐ Psalm 138
☐ Psalm 139

DEVOTIONAL THOUGHT

Read John 15:12-17

We generally view love and friendship from the perspective of the receiver. We evaluate our relationships based on what they bring to us. Perhaps this is why so many marriages don't last and friendships whither in the wind. The moment a challenge arises or they cost us a little too much they can be viewed as more trouble than they are worth.

But authentic love looks out for the other. A loving relationship is one in which we give, serve, and care regardless of what is flowing back. Great love is one that sacrifices for the other. True love is one that elevates the other. We often think of this in the instant, take-a-bullet-for-you sense. Exceptional love is also willing to walk the road of slow, steady, sacrifice that sets aside one's own well-being in favor of the other.

Are you willing to lay down your life for your family, friend, spouse, child, or neighbor? Reflect on the sacrificial love of Christ this week. He did not just serve you for the day He went to the cross. He spent a lifetime serving, pointing humans towards the Kingdom, offering life, and giving of Himself that you might find forgiveness. This love is something that happens in the small moments and is also a conscious, repeated decision overtime to put others above you.

REFLECT

Do you focus more on what you give or what you receive in relationships? What does that reveal about you?

Reflect on a time when someone sacrificed their time, energy, finances, wellbeing, or status for you. How impactful was that?

Think back to a time when you sacrificed for someone else. Consider the blessings that emerged from it. Rejoice at how God worked through you!

How might you sacrificially love the people God has put in your life? Are you willing to love your neighbors even when it costs you something?

MY WEEKLY GOALS

Jot down goals & activities for the week.

Love God

This week I will love God by:

☐

☐

☐

☐

☐

Love Neighbor

This week I will love my neighbors by:

☐

☐

☐

☐

☐

PRAISE & PRAYERS

Daily Prayers

Each morning and evening pray the daily prayers.

Praise

God, this week I praise you for:

☐

☐

☐

Personal Prayers

God, please move in these areas of my life this week:

☐

☐

☐

Prayers for Others

God, this week please move in the following neighbors lives:

☐

☐

☐

JOURNAL

IMITATE GOD'S LOVE

Date: _____

VERSE OF THE WEEK

Therefore be imitators of God, as beloved children, and live in love, as Christ loved us and gave himself up for us, a fragrant offering and sacrifice to God.

Ephesians 5:1-2

READING PLAN

- ☐ 1 John 5
- ☐ 2 John 1
- ☐ 3 John 1

- ☐ Revelation 1
- ☐ Revelation 2
- ☐ Revelation 3

- ☐ Psalm 140
- ☐ Psalm 141
- ☐ Psalm 142

DEVOTIONAL THOUGHT

Read Ephesians 4:17-5:2

It has been said that "*imitation is the sincerest form of flattery.*" If we really love our God and praise Him the way He deserves, we will find ourselves imitating Him. As we find ourselves imitating Him, we find ourselves living in love.

To live in love is to give of ourselves for the good of others just as Christ did. To live in love is to respond to the love that God the Father first bestowed upon us. To live in love is to worship God not just with our words but with all that we do.

How would you describe your imitation of God? Is it something that you just engage in sometimes? Is it something that you only do in front of a crowd or when at church? How might you take the next step towards an all-encompassing living in love?

REFLECT

Do you imitate God? In what ways? How frequently?

Do you consider your love for others as a reflection of your love for God?

Do you consider your love for others as a reflection of God to them?

What are some ways that you can imitate God by loving others this week? Remember that beyond the actions themselves, these are reflections of your love for God and His love for others.

MY WEEKLY GOALS

Jot down goals & activities for the week.

Love God

This week I will love God by:

☐

☐

☐

☐

☐

Love Neighbor

This week I will love my neighbors by:

☐

☐

☐

☐

☐

PRAISE & PRAYERS

Daily Prayers
Each morning and evening pray the daily prayers.

Praise
God, this week I praise you for:

☐

☐

☐

Personal Prayers
God, please move in these areas of my life this week:

☐

☐

☐

Prayers for Others
God, this week please move in the following neighbors lives:

☐

☐

☐

JOURNAL

LOVING THOSE THAT ARE DIFFERENT

Date: _____

VERSE OF THE WEEK

Thus says the Lord of hosts: Render true judgments, show kindness and mercy to one another; do not oppress the widow, the orphan, the alien, or the poor; and do not devise evil in your hearts against one another.

ZECHARIAH 7:9-10

READING PLAN

- ☐ Revelation 4
- ☐ Revelation 5
- ☐ Revelation 6
- ☐ Revelation 7:1-8:5
- ☐ Revelation 8:6-9:21
- ☐ Revelation 10
- ☐ Psalm 143
- ☐ Psalm 144
- ☐ Psalm 145

DEVOTIONAL THOUGHT

Read Zechariah 7:8-14

Since the earliest days of history, the marginalized have been among us. Borders were drawn. Barriers were erected. We found ways of excluding those that did not nicely fit.

In the time of Moses, these people were the widows, orphans, immigrants, and the needy. Immigrants were particularly dangerous as they threatened culture and faith and it was unclear if they were trustworthy at all. Nonetheless, God called them to love and care for all the outsiders. Whereas many would have expelled them from their land, the neighbor-loving approach was to welcome them with open arms, care for their needs, and treat them compassionately. Whether they looked, spoke, or acted the same, the people of God were commanded to care for the marginalized. Yes, they were different. No, they could not always contribute in the standard ways. But God loved them and charged His people to model His own love and care.

411

Who do you attempt to exclude - whether through direct action or through indirectly sanctioned efforts? Examine yourself honestly. Start with any groups of people you dislike. Setting aside differences, politics, and rationalizations, ask yourself how your merciful Savior would treat these people. Now ask yourself what you ought to do differently.

REFLECT

What people are most hated or forgotten in society? What is the impact on their wellbeing?

Do you struggle with loving immigrants? The poor? The homeless? Different ethnicities? Those in prison? Some other group of people? Why?

How would Jesus treat them? How does the Lord call you to love them?

Think of those you struggle to love? How do you justify it? Rationalizations aside, God is calling you to love the marginalized and those different from you no matter what. But, will you?

MY WEEKLY GOALS

Jot down goals & activities for the week.

Love God

This week I will love God by:

☐

☐

☐

☐

☐

Love Neighbor

This week I will love my neighbors by:

☐

☐

☐

☐

☐

PRAISE & PRAYERS

Daily Prayers

Each morning and evening pray the daily prayers.

Praise

God, this week I praise you for:

☐

☐

☐

Personal Prayers

God, please move in these areas of my life this week:

☐

☐

☐

Prayers for Others

God, this week please move in the following neighbors lives:

☐

☐

☐

JOURNAL

DELIGHT IN THE LORD

Date: _____

VERSE OF THE WEEK

Take delight in the Lord, and he will give you the desires of your heart.

PSALM 37:4

READING PLAN

☐ Revelation 11	☐ Revelation 14	☐ Psalm 146
☐ Revelation 12	☐ Revelation 15	☐ Psalm 147
☐ Revelation 13	☐ Revelation 16	☐ Psalm 148

DEVOTIONAL THOUGHT

Read Psalm 37

What do you delight in? Family? A sport or hobby? Tacos or some other food? A favorite movie? Art or music?

Would you say you delight in the Lord? This might seem like an odd question to many. To enjoy yourself or delight in the Lord is to celebrate who He is and what He has done. Just like eating a portion of delicious food or partaking in an enjoyable hobby can take our focus off of other things, delighting in the Lord can transport us into His presence. As we are caught up in His majesty, our hearts are drawn to Him, our will is aligned with His, and our ways become transformed into His ways. Our desires become one with God's will and, as a result, we see them realized.

Set your focus on the grandeur and marvelous acts of God this week. Admire them. Rejoice in them. Delight yourself in them.

REFLECT

What foods, toys, entertainment, experiences, or other things do you most delight in? What do you find enjoyable about them?

Do you delight in the Lord like you delight in earthly things?

Do you make opportunities to reflect on the Lord and His goodness? Do you see a correlation between how much time you focus on God and how much you enjoy Him?

Do you want to enjoy Jesus more? If so, what would it take to make time and space for that?

MY WEEKLY GOALS

Jot down goals & activities for the week.

Love God

This week I will love God by:

☐

☐

☐

☐

☐

Love Neighbor

This week I will love my neighbors by:

☐

☐

☐

☐

☐

PRAISE & PRAYERS

Daily Prayers
Each morning and evening pray the daily prayers.

Praise
God, this week I praise you for:

☐

☐

☐

Personal Prayers
God, please move in these areas of my life this week:

☐

☐

☐

Prayers for Others
God, this week please move in the following neighbors lives:

☐

☐

☐

JOURNAL

COMMISSIONING

Date: _____

VERSE OF THE WEEK

Go therefore and make disciples of all nations, baptizing them in the name of the Father and of the Son and of the Holy Spirit, and teaching them to obey everything that I have commanded you. And remember, I am with you always, to the end of the age.

MATTHEW 28:19-20

READING PLAN

- ☐ Revelation 17
- ☐ Revelation 18
- ☐ Revelation 19
- ☐ Revelation 20
- ☐ Revelation 21:1-22:5
- ☐ Revelation 22:6-21
- ☐ Psalm 149
- ☐ Psalm 150

DEVOTIONAL THOUGHT

Read Matthew 28:16-20

The end of the gospel of Matthew does not contain a goodbye so much as a commencement. While this was the end of Jesus' earthly ministry and of the years of the disciples' apprenticeship with Him, it was merely the beginning of their ministry adventures. This passage which has been deemed "*the Great Commission*" launches the disciples into a new era in which, with the Holy Spirit working through them, they would be the instruments through whom God continued His mission here on earth.

This commission was not just for the disciples of Jesus who literally followed Him around on earth. It was first to them but continues on to all who would follow Him in the centuries afterward and still today. If you consider yourself to be Jesus' follower, you too are sent into all the world (starting in the city you live in and extending to the far ends of the earth) filled with such a love for your neighbor that you would make disciples of them, baptize them and teach them the ways of Jesus.

Three things advance this mission. First, you must love God and be aligned with Him. Second, you must love humans and desire that they experience God's grace, love, mercy, and hope to such a degree that it propels you into motion. Lastly, Jesus - who with good reason was named Emmanuel meaning "God is with us" - goes with you wherever and whenever and works in, through, and around you to accomplish the mission.

This journal, similarly, is not meant to be the end of the road for you. Rather, it is a tool along the journey that is intended to help push you forward and mobilize you.

You have been commissioned by Jesus to (1) love God with all your heart, soul, and strength and (2) love your neighbor as yourself. Will you respond to the call and go out on a mission?

May you fall more deeply in love with the Almighty God and reflect His immense love for the entire world.

REFLECT

Do you view yourself as a key contributor to God's mission to reconcile people to Him? Why or why not?

Do you know that God is with you on your mission to love others? Do you invite Him into that mission or do you attempt to do it on your own?

You have been commissioned by Jesus. Will you respond?

MY WEEKLY GOALS

Jot down goals & activities for the week.

Love God

This week I will love God by:

☐

☐

☐

☐

☐

Love Neighbor

This week I will love my neighbors by:

☐

☐

☐

☐

☐

PRAISE & PRAYERS

Daily Prayers
Each morning and evening pray the daily prayers.

Praise
God, this week I praise you for:

☐

☐

☐

Personal Prayers
God, please move in these areas of my life this week:

☐

☐

☐

Prayers for Others
God, this week please move in the following neighbors lives:

☐

☐

☐

JOURNAL

NEIGHBOR
PRAYER LIST

This year I am praying that God would move in the lives of:

1.

2.

3.

4.

5.

6.

7.

8.

9.

10.

IDEAS FOR LOVING NEIGHBORS

May the following ideas spark Kingdom creativity in you as you consider how you might love others.

Do not merely rely on the ideas presented here. Listen for where Jesus is leading. Pray for those that you interact with and petition God to transform your heart. Remember that the goal is not just to perform acts of service but to develop authentic relationships, to learn to love neighbors, and to reflect God's love to others.

▶ Learn the names and stories of others. You cannot truly love your neighbor if you do not know your neighbor.

▶ Invite someone to coffee or a meal. Ask about and listen to what is going on in their life.

▶ Help a neighbor with some yard work. Chat while you work.

▶ Throw a party. Be intentional to learn the names, stories, and needs of your neighbors.

▶ Visit someone who is sick. Bring them medicine or a meal.

▶ Help a co-worker with some work they are struggling with. Go above and beyond your responsibilities to sincerely support another.

▶ Work an extra shift at work and donate the funds to someone in need.

▶ Get lunch for a homeless person. Do not just buy lunch and drop it off. Ask for their order, pick up food for both of you, and then eat together. Discover more about them as you eat. Offer to pray for them and continue doing even after the meal together.

▶ Offer to tutor a neighbor.

▶ Volunteer to serve in a local school.

▶ Buy some canned goods and donate to a local food bank or shelter. Ask if there are any other needs or if they could use volunteers. Get to know those you are serving where possible.

▶ Learn how to change a tire (if you do not know already). Help those you come across by offering to lend a hand.

▶ Cook extra food when you make a meal or bake. Bless someone with it.

▶ Visit a neighbor in the hospital. Offer to pray for them. Check in on them afterwards.

▶ Offer to babysit so that a neighbor can have time to go on a date, run an errand or even so that they might simply take a break.

▶ Purchase a cup of coffee for the person in line behind you. Use the opportunity to train yourself to view your resources as belonging to a purpose greater than your own consumption.

▶ Organize a group of people to respond to a global disaster through monetary donations or more tangible support.

▶ Give a neighbor a ride to a doctor's appointment or the hospital. Don't wait for someone to ask. Offer to be a help in times of need.

▶ Go on a missions trip to build a home or to serve in some other way. Pay attention to the people you are assisting. Build a relationship that goes beyond the task at hand.

▶ Feeling hurt or wronged by someone? Let that frustration mobilize you to pray for and forgive that person. Forgive them as Christ forgave you. Pray that you might love them even while you do not feel it is merited.

▶ Walk around your neighborhood, praying as you go. Ask God to open your eyes to see the people and the things that weigh on them. Ask Him to mold your heart so that you might love them more deeply. Pray that He would move in powerful ways and that He might use you to reach those in the community.

▶ Help teach English (or your local language) to an immigrant. Develop a relationship in the process. Pray that God would help you with the call to welcome the stranger and that you would learn to love this neighbor more genuinely.

CELEBRATION LIST

CELEBRATION LIST

This year, I celebrate God for the following ways that I have seen Him move in my life and in the lives of those around me:

1.

2.

3.

4.

5.

6.

7.

8.

9.

10.

11.

12.

13.

14.

15.

16.

17.

18.

19.

20.

21.

22.

23.

24.

25.

WHERE TO GO
FROM HERE

Congratulations on working through 52 weeks of devotions! I hope that you have deepened your love for God and for others as a result. May this have a lasting impact on your ability to walk in the footsteps of Jesus.

While you may have completed this journal, loving God and neighbors is not a destination you arrive at. It is a journey that you embark on. There will be continued challenges, obstacles, and distractions. If you're not careful, some of those old ways will try to creep back in. Continue on towards the goal.

We, humans, are forgetful people. We tend to slide back into our old ways. This was key when the first component of the Great Commandment was originally given to Israel.

> *"Hear, O Israel: The Lord is our God, the Lord alone. You shall love the Lord your God with all your heart, and with all your soul, and with all your might. Keep these words that I am commanding you today in your heart. Recite them to your children and talk about them when you are at home and when you are away, when you lie down and when you rise. Bind them as a sign on your hand, fix them as an emblem on your forehead, and write them on the doorposts of your house and on your gates."* Deuteronomy 6:4-9

Not only was the command given to love God with our entire being, but it was followed up by a series of practices to keep it top of mind. Reciting these words morning and night, home or away implies that whenever and wherever you find yourself, you should concentrate on these ideas. Using them on apparel and decorations meant that they were unavoidable. The purpose was to ensure that the people would always be reminded of these ideas that were to be the lens through which they viewed the world.

As you continue on toward the prize, keep these commands before you. Wear them on your wrist. Decorate your home with them. Place them on your desk or in your kitchen. Do not let a day go by when you do not reflect on your love for the Almighty God and for those around you.

Some other ways you might continue on would be to explore the spiritual disciplines, commit to praying for a list of neighbors every day, or committing to reading the entire Bible over the next year. I highly recommend that you write out a plan for how you will love God and neighbor in the coming weeks, months, and year. Revisit the plan to ensure you are following through.

You can also consider working through this journal again. You could work through it each year allowing God to speak to you in fresh ways and addressing either new or continued challenges. You could use a generic journal for your notes if you did not want a fresh copy.

No matter which approach you choose to take, continue forward toward the goal. If you were to ask Jesus today what the greatest commandment for your life was, He would tell you to love God and love neighbors. **If this is the essence of what He is calling you to, is it not of the utmost importance to respond to?**

Be neither complacent nor overwhelmed. I quite understand that this is very challenging. However, it is worth pursuing. Our created purpose and our response to God's love should propel us towards this. Moreover, Jesus promises that He is with us always. Remember that Emmanuel walks by your side and His Spirit is there to give you the strength.

The commandment is clear: love God and love your neighbor.

Will you continue to respond?

Made in the USA
Las Vegas, NV
05 February 2021